Nizhny Novgorod

Welcome!

Нижний Новгород

Добро пожаловать!

Printed and published by
BoD - Books on Demand, Norderstedt
ISBN 978-3-7460-2869-9

TABLE OF CONTENTS

MUSEUMS, ART AND CULTURE 52

NIGHT LIFE   82

Introduction

With almost 1,25 million inhabitants Nizhny Novgorod is the fifth-largest city in Russia. From 1932-1990 the city was named Gorky, after the well-known author who was born there. The view of the confluence of the Oka and the Volga is breathtaking. There is probably no comparable European city in which one can

enjoy such an unobstructed view to the horizon from the centre of the city. At this sight one gets a feeling for the Russian expanse and the size of this country. Nizhny is a large city due to the population, but rather a province, compared to the large metropolises of Moscow and St. Petersburg. This is also shown by the fact that Nizhny is poorly developed for tourism which is particularly problematic for foreigners without knowledge of Russian. This city guide is directed primarily, but of course not only, to people who travel to Nizhny Novgorod for a longer period of time. I lived in Nizhny from 2012 until 2016 and I would like to share my experiences with others, so that you also get to know and love this beautiful city.

History of the City

1221	Founded by Yuri II (1189-1238), Grand Prince of Vladimir
from 1392	Part of the Grand Duchy of Moscow
15th century	Fortress in the fight against the Kazan Tartars
17th century	Center of resistance against Poland and Sweden
1612	Assembly of the People's Army under Minin and Pozharsky at the Kremlin, from where they made their way to Moscow to expel the Polish armies (great painting in the Art Museum)
1781	Nizhny gets its coat of arms. For more information, please visit: *http://www.admgor.nnov.ru/en/nizhniy-novgorod/symbols/*
19th century	Important trade center between Europe and Asia
1817	The exhibition will be moved from Makaryev to Nizhny
1932-1990	The city was named "Gorky" after Maxim Gorky (1868-1936), who was born in Nizhny
Time of the Soviet Union	Development to the industrial center - important branches of industry, e.g. The automobile plant GAZ. Closed city - not available for foreigners, due to the armaments industry (nuclear submarines, combat aircraft and tanks)
1991	The city is again opened to foreigners.

today	Nizhny is the capital of the same-named Oblast (Region). The governor is Valery Shantsev, the Mayor – Ivan Karnilin

Holidays and Celebrations

January 1-5   New Year Holidays

January 6-7   Orthodox Christmas

In the Russian Orthodox Church, the old Julian calendar is still observed, which means that Christmas is not celebrated until January. In the time of the Soviet Union it was forbidden to celebrate Christmas. This changed only with the disintegration of the Soviet Union.

February 23   Day of the Defender of the Fatherland

The origins of this holiday date back to the beginning of the 20th century. It was then the Day of the Red Army. Since 2002, this holiday has been officially reintroduced to honor the members of the Russian armed forces. But in the younger generation it is more likely to be celebrated as a men's day.

March 8   Women's Day

An important holiday in Russia where women get flowers and other gifts.

Easter

Due to the different calendars, Easter holidays have different days in Russia. However, in the church only the night of Saturday is celebrated with long worship services on Easter Sunday.

May 1   Labour Day

May 9   Victory over Hitler's Germany

This is probably the most important holiday in Russia and is celebrated with great military parades (see "Important Information – Georgian ribbon").

June 12	The Day of Russia
	Since 1992 official holiday. Across the population, however, the holiday is of little importance.
November 4	National Unity Day
	Since 2005 an official holiday. For Nizhny of special importance, because of the departure of Minin and Pozharsky's national army to Moscow in 1612, which ended the Russian-Polish war.
December 31	New Year
	New Year's Eve is celebrated in Russia like Christmas with fir trees, Ded Moroz (Father Frost, the Russian Santa Clause), gifts and only with the family. On the other hand, the actual Christian Christmas festivity has little significance for the general public. After the October Revolution in 1917 the Christian Christmas celebration was forbidden. The related traditions, however, were moved to New Year's Eve.

If a public holiday falls on a weekend, it is postponed to the next working day. For this reason, holiday regulations are a little different each year. There is usually a long vacation period after New Year and in May. Some working days are therefore changed so it might be necessary to work on Saturday. On public holidays the shops are not closed.

Important Information

AIR CONDITIONING/HEATING

You may be thinking: "Why do I need an air-conditioning system? It's winter half the year!" In fact, the summer can get quite hot, and you will be grateful for air conditioning. However, the air-conditioning system is even more useful in spring and autumn, as it is also used for heating during the transition times to the heating periods. In Russia there are state-controlled heating periods, i.e., the heating is centrally controlled and you usually have no influence on it. This is why you are lucky if you have a thermostat - you can switch off the radiators so that you do not have to adjust the temperature of the apartment in winter by opening the windows. Also, make sure that your apartment is equipped with a boiler, since once a year for a few days the hot water is switched off. The regulation of indoor heating is supposedly based on the outside temperature. Buildings are usually heated from October to May.

CAR RENTAL

The big, international car rental companies have finally made it to Nizhny. You can rent a car from Avis, Europcar or Hertz at the train station and at the airport. Unfortunately, it is often not possible to rent the car in one Russian city and return it in another.

CAR TOWING

The parking situation is precarious in the inner city, as there is hardly any public parking. As a result, towing companies are very profitable. Since there are no traffic wardens, your car is towed away with every offense. It is expensive and extremely time consuming to get your car back. If your car has been towed, call the following telephone number: 417 17 07. You will find out which car lot your car is located in. Write down the address and go there. You will receive a certificate. Then go to the police (Delovaya Street 3) to pay the penalty. Only then can you go back to the car lot - of course at the other end of the city - to reclaim your car. The towing company requires about 2000 rubles. For the taxi ride you should plan about 1000 rubles. The fine is usually the lightest part of the experience.

DOORBELL/INTERCOM

Similar to the mailbox, there are no names on the bell to your apartment. So visitors need to know the number of your apartment. Usually the bell/ringers are next to the main door. Visitors should select the number of your apartment and then press "B".

DRIVING

Driving is basically manageable in Nizhny, but dangerous. The road conditions are extremely bad. You must pay attention to the road to avoid enormous potholes. Drivers tend to be aggressive. For this reason, there are many accidents. Many cars are equipped with video cameras, in order to reconstruct the accident. In recent years, more inhabitants are able to afford a car, which leads to too much traffic and congestion at peak times. On the weekends, when the city dwellers drive to their dacha, there is congestion at the major arteries. In urban areas, the speed limit is 60 km/h, except for occasional 90 km/h zones. You should stick to the limits, since there are speed cameras everywhere.

EMERGENCY CALLS

Emergency Service Center 01 (from mobile phone 112), Police 02 and Medical Emergency Service 03.

FLOOR NUMBERING IN BUILDINGS

In Russia the ground floor is considered the first floor, and elevators have no "0", and start with "1".

GEORGIAN RIBBON – MAY 9TH

In cars and shops, on backpacks and handbags, the Georgian ribbon is now omnipresent. With its two orange and three black stripes, it stands for the pride of an entire nation, not only for the victory over Hitler's Germany. The origin of the Georgian ribbon dates to the 18th century, where it was first awarded in Russia as a military order. It is named after St. George, who died as a martyr for the defense of the Christian faith. World War II is still very present in today's Russian generation. Russia is also doing a lot to ensure that the "great victory" is not forgotten. A part of this is the Georgian ribbon, which since 2005 is distributed among the people in May. On May 9, a large military parade takes place on Minin Square. Passing tanks in the inner city and the sight of military strength is disconcerting. You can see the inscription "To Berlin" on some cars. Children are much more familiar with the military. Thus, war equipment is displayed in the centre of the Kremlin, which the children use as climbing frames, and balloons in the shape of armaments are sold there. A Russian woman once told me that the memory of the glorious "Great Patriotic War" is the only thing that still unites the Russian people.

INTERNATIONAL ASSOCIATION - EXPATS

ICANN stands for "International Community Association Nizhny Novgorod" and is a federation of international companies in Nizhny. Currently, there are about 40 members, including ThyssenKrupp, Liebherr and Volkswagen among others. But private individuals can also become members. Generally, the expat community is accessible. If you want to get to know new people, the "international table" is recommended once a month. The organization is managed by a board of directors who, according to the statutes, must be foreigners, and are usually the managing directors of one of the large companies. In addition, there are two permanent members of staff, who maintain contacts for the city and organize meetings. There is also a wide range of social events and excursions.

http://icann-nn.ru/main.html

MAILBOX

There is no name on your residential mailbox, but only the number of the apartment. Mailboxes are installed in the corridor and not outside the building. International mail does arrive eventually, but letters and packages take at least four weeks. If you are expecting a package, you will find a pick-up ticket in your mailbox. Then you must either go to the **main post office** (Bolshaya Pokrovskaya 56 - Большая Покровская улица, 56) and pick it up by presenting your identity card, or call the number on the ticket so that a courier will deliver the package at a suitable time.

MOBILE PHONE/INTERNET

There are three major mobile phone providers in Nizhny: Beeline, Megafon and MTS. Contracts can be concluded on the Internet as well as at their stores. For private users, often only prepaid contracts are offered. You must then regularly charge your phone. This can be done either on the Internet, if you have a Russian account, or at certain terminals, e.g., in almost any supermarket. Internet for the mobile phone is relatively cheap. If you travel a lot in Russia, be sure to choose a Russia-wide tariff, otherwise calling outside the Nizhny Novgorod region is as expensive as an international call. In many restaurants there is also free wi-fi. The largest fixed line provider is Rostelekom.

MOSQUITOS

Mosquitos come with spring melt. May and June are usually the worst months. After that it is at least better in the city. For this reason, it is recommended to use fly screens and have insect spray with you. In recent years, however, it has been noted that the number of mosquitos has decreased.

ORTHODOX CHRUCH

The Russian "state religion" is Orthodox Christianity. The cityscape is characterized by magnificent churches, which are usually open daily and freely accessible. Women should note that they have to wear head cover. Sometimes you also have to wear a skirt. However, scarves are often available at the entrance. Unlike a Catholic or Protestant church, there is no seating, but during the entire service, the church stands, which can be several hours during high celebrations. The churches are usually very ornate outside and decorated inside. In the Orthodox Church, icons - portraits of saints - play an important role. When visiting a church, the believers go through the church, kiss different icons, usually light a candle and cross themselves several times, before exiting the church. Unlike in the Catholic Church, they make the sign of the cross from the right to the left shoulder. If you would like to attend a church service, you should take a local church-

goer, since otherwise the liturgy will not be understood. Another difference is the **cross** in the Orthodox church. The upper, additional bar symbolizes the sign on which the INRI inscription was located. The lower oblique bar represents the board on which Jesus had to place his feet.

PHARMACY

Many medications are available without a prescription. A pharmacy (аптека) can be found at almost every corner. Pharmacies are partially open 24 hours a day. It is recommended to buy only known medications. In Russia it is customary to get a list of medicines from the doctor after a doctor's visit, according to the motto "the more the better".

PUBLIC TRANSPORT

The public transport network is very well developed. There are buses, metro, marshrutkas, trams, trolleybuses (high-buses) and regional trains (Elektrichka). The marshrutkas are minibuses in private hands. They do not automatically pick you up at every stop, so you have to lift your hand and signal them. When you want to get off, you need to push a button by the door. All transport within the city costs 28 rubles. It is paid directly - either to the driver or to the conductor (conductor). The Russian version of Google is Yandex. Via Yandex Maps (also available as an app) you can plan the route and see the available means of transport.

https://maps.yandex.ru/47/nizhny-novgorod/

REGISTRATION

If you do not have a permanent residence permit or special visa, you are obliged to register with the local immigration authority within seven working days upon arrival. Even if you have a multiple entry visa, registration is necessary after each entry if you are in Russia for more than seven days. Typically, registration by your inviting company or in any hotel will be automatic. In addition, it is possible to register with the post office, which then forwards the form to the migration authority.

SAFETY

Nizhny is a safe city, if you follow, as in every city, certain basic rules. In the center, the police presence is high and one can go for a walk even after it gets dark without any problem. The urban areas further outside, especially Avtozavod area, should be avoided.

SOCIAL NETWORKS

Although many Russians have a Facebook account, the Russian variant "Vkontakte" is much more popular and frequented. Most of the restaurants or events in Nizhny have their own groups within this network.

https://vk.com/

TAP WATER

Do not drink tap water in Russia. Some apartments, however, have built-in filters in the sink. Many buy drinking water in large plastic bottles in the supermarket. Certain companies offer a water delivery service home.

TAXI

Taxis are relatively cheap. There are official taxis with meters everywhere in the city. You can also order a taxi by telephone (e.g., Novoe Taxi: +7 (831) 4-216-116). Rutaxi (+7 (831) 215-55-55), which offer private rides with their own car and are much cheaper. You call the control call center and make a request. The price will be communicated immediately. A text message with the number plate and type of car is then sent. If you do not speak Russian, you can also order a taxi from Rutaxi or TapTaxi via internet or an app by entering the address. The taxi will usually arrive within 15 minutes, depending on the time of the day. You can also specify a specific time, for example, if you need an airport transfer.

http://nnovgorod.rutaxi.ru/en/index.html

TIME ZONE/DAYLIGHT SAVING TIME

The time zone is UTC+3. The time is not changed in Russia.

TOURIST INFORMATION CENTER

The first tourist information center in Nizhny opened in November 2012. It is located near the ship dock. The website is available in English and gives you an initial overview.

Opening hours: 9:00 am to 6:00 pm Monday-Friday

Phone: +7 (831) 272-71-72

Address: Nizhnevolzhskaya Naberezhnaya 6ж

http://en.nnwelcome.ru/

TRAVEL GUIDE APP

If you are looking for a travel guide app for your smartphone, then "NNovgorod" is recommended. This is, however, only available through Russian iTunes.

https://itunes.apple.com/ru/app/nnovgorod/id622580334?mt=8

WASTE SEPARATION

Waste separation is unknown in Russia. All waste ends in the same bin, whether glass, paper, plastic or waste. Although there are now groups that are advocating for recycling, the system is still missing. Even if you do separate your garbage, what good is it if it all ends up in the same garbage dump? However, there are separate acceptance points for paper and beer bottles. Empty batteries can be taken to MediaMarkt and IKEA. You can find all information on this topic in the following Vkontakte group: *https://vk.com/razdelno_nn*.

WEATHER

The conventional wisdom is that Russia is only cold, of course. It is true that the winter is more severe and can go down to -25 °C, but one is rewarded with beautiful snow, and it is impressive to see the Volga river completely frozen. In general, spring and autumn are quite short. Winter usually lasts from October to March. But you can also look forward to a nice summer with temperatures up to +30 °C.

Arrival and Departure

AIR

If you land at the airport "Strigino" for the first time, you get the impression of a small town, as there are few flights per day and there are hardly any flights abroad. The international airport abbreviation is GOJ. The new airport was opened in 2016. An overview of the destinations from Nizhny can be found on the website below. Aeroflot, S7 and UTair, for example, fly to Moscow. The airport is about 1 hour by car from the city center, depending on the traffic situation. A taxi from Nizhny Kremlin costs about 500 rubles if you order it by telephone (see above "important information"). There are official taxis that use meters. With these taxis the trip costs about 800 rubles. The taxi stand at the airport also provides child seats. If you decide to travel with one of the taxi drivers who approach you, make sure you agree on the price in advance to avoid nasty surprises.

http://www.airportnn.ru/en/passazhiram

BUS

There are four bus stations in Nizhny (Kanavinskaya, Sennaya, Sherbinki and Avtovokzal "Nizhegorodsky"). It should be mentioned that one could also go by bus to Moscow, but the bus is inferior next to the other means of transport.

CAR

You will miss modern highways. The roads are in poor shape and the traffic network might not be what you are used to. Between Moscow and Nizhny there is a highway, the M7. However, the drive is very unpredictable and can also take 8 hours for only 400 km.

GROUP TAXI

From the train station you can take a small bus to Moscow. The meeting point is the parking lot opposite the station in front of the McDonalds. With about 900 rubles, this is the cheapest, but one of the most uncomfortable, ways to go to Moscow. The ticket is bought directly from the driver.

TRAIN

The most popular way to travel in Russia is by train. This is also the most comfortable way to go to Moscow. Arrival is in the east of the city at Kursky station (Курский вокзал). The fastest and most comfortable train is called "Strizh" which takes only 3:45 hours. In the train you can buy an internet access for 99 rubles. The Siemens train "Lastochka" takes about 4 hours. Tickets can be bought at travel agencies, train stations, or on the Internet (if you buy the tickets on the Internet, it has to be printed out). You cannot exchange tickets purchased on the Internet. You can cancel the ticket online, but for a small fee, and hope that the money will be credited to your card within one month. In order to cancel tickets, you must first update their status, then a special button will appear. Do not forget your passport when you are travelling, as this must always be displayed when you board the train. Each wagon has its own conductor. A ticket to Moscow costs about 2000 rubles. You can search for train connections and buy tickets on the following website:

http://pass.rzd.ru/main-pass/public/en.

Sights

There is much to discover in Nizhny. I recommend you just stroll through the Old Town and explore the charms of the city on your own, as there is a historic building on almost every street, nestled between new buildings and almost dilapidated old wooden houses. The following is an alphabetical listing of the main sights of Nizhny Novgorod:

ALEXANDER NEVSKY CATHEDRAL

The large, yellow cathedral directly on the Strelka is one of the landmarks of Nizhny, as it is visible from many spots. It was

designed by the architects R. Kivelein and L. Dal, and built between 1864 and 1881. With its height of 87 meters, it is one of the largest churches in Russia. In 1929, the church was closed and an air defense gun was installed in one of the gables to defend the city from air raids. The entire interior decoration, including the frescoes, was damaged by several fires in the 1940s. Lengthy reconstruction began in 1991.

Address: Strelka 3a (ул. Стрелка, д. 3a)

http://nevskiy-nne.ru/

Close to the Cathedral, on the old harbour area, a new football stadium for the World Cup 2018 is being built.

BLAGOVESHENSKY MONASTERY

From the direction of the Alexander Nevsky Cathedral, take the first bridge (Kanavinsky Most / Канавинский мост), and you can see the oldest monastery of the city, the Blagoveshensky Monastery

(Благовещенский Монастырь). Its origins lie in the 13th century. It was built to protect the river crossing at the Oka River. However, the buildings that can be seen today go back to the 17th century. The monastery consists of several churches. In the center stands the Annunciation Cathedral with its black domes and striking arches. Close to the Cathedral are the Church of the Assumption of the Virgin with striking blue towers, a bell tower, a dining hall and the former monk's cells. On the other side of the Cathedral, the Alexevskaya Church with its columned entrances shines in the new, golden splendor of the restored domes. It was built in the 19th century by host pilgrims due to the growing importance of the fair in Nizhny. Between this Church and the Cathedral, there is also a monastery hospital. The monastery is at the same time the seat of the **theological seminary** (Нижегородская духовная семинария), with its own small library and an exhibition space. Visits to the small museum must be arranged by telephone (430-50-64).

Address: Pokhvalinsky syezd 5 (Похвалинский съезд, д. 5)

http://nds.nne.ru/

Along the Oka, below the monastery, lies a forgotten city quarter. It was built at the same time as the monastery and served as its "suburb", which explains why it was subordinated to the monastery. It was not until the end of the 18th century that it became a district of Nizhny. Unfortunately, many houses need renovation, but a stroll along the Oka is worthwhile in any case,

if you want to move away from the main points of interest and the bustle of the city (Chernigovskaya Street / Черниговская улица). On your itinerary you will discover some beautiful 19th-century residences. At the end of the road you will come across an industrial site with a disused mill. There are some photo studios there available for rent. When you walk under the metro bridge, you will come directly to the beautifully restored former railway station building of the Moscow-Kazan railway from the beginning of the 20th century. Today the building is used for offices. Continue along the dirt road and you will come across a large, old railway station ruin on the left. Opposite at the embankment of the Oka is an old water tower with interesting **graffiti**.

BOLSHAYA POKROVSKAYA

The Bolshaya Pokrovskaya (Большая Покровская) Street is the

main pedestrian zone of the city. It leads from Minin Square to Gorky Square and is blocked for motorists. Even though more and more shops are moving to major shopping centers, the Bolshaya Pokrovskaya is popular among the locals, especially because of the many restaurants. These invite you to sit outside in the summer to listen to the street musicians or to observe the passing walkers.

If you start your walk from Minin Square, past the building of the **former city parliament**, the entrance to the **market** (мытный рынок) will be about 50m further on the left hand side under a corrugated iron roof. There you can buy fresh fruit and vegetables. A look at the meat market is also worth it, just for interest. Whether it corresponds to hygiene standards - especially in the summer months – is another question.

A little further on is the Theater Square with the **Drama Theater**. The building dates back to the end of the 19th century. To the right is a monument to Nikolai A. **Dobrolubov** (1836-1861), a Russian literary scholar who was born in Nizhny. If you want to know more about  him, visit the **Dobrolubov Museum** (see "Museums, Art and Culture" below), the family's home.

Just before the tram crosses the Bolshaya Pokrovskaya, the **Court** of the Nizhny Novgorod region lies on the right hand in a U-shaped building. Across the street is the former building of the nobility meeting with its six white pillars, which today houses the Sverdlov **Cultural Center**. Various events and courses take place here - for example a ballet for children or the service of the Evangelical **Vineyard community** on Sundays at 11:30 am. In the premises there is also a **ticket booth** from Kassir.ru and an **exhibition of exotic animals and reptiles**. Not far from the cultural center, after crossing the street on the left behind the kiosk, is a **monument** to **Y. M. Sverdlov** (1885-1919). Sverdlov was also born in Nizhny and was a politician and revolutionary.

Probably the most imposing building of the pedestrian zone is the **State Bank** - now the branch of the Russian Central Bank in Nizhny Novgorod. The bank was built on the occasion of the 300-year Romanov regency and seems to have sprung from a fairy tale movie. The interiors match the fanciful exterior as well. Unfortunately, a visit is only

possible with a special guide, or once a year for the Open Day.

Follow the Bolshaya Pokrovskaya further uphill towards Gorky Square, and you will see a small green area on the right. Behind it is a building belonging to **Lobachevsky University**. It is the largest university in the city. Here occasionally concerts take place in the large hall on the second floor.

Along the adjacent fence in the next side street, the local **painters** offer their works. Here you can buy beautiful oil paintings of the city by local artists.

On the next corner is the first cinema of the city, which still houses a cinema (Cinema Orlyonok). Next to it is the **Puppet Theater**, and a little further down is the largest **souvenir shop** in the city with traditional craftsmanship of the region. On the fourth floor, the building also houses a lovingly furnished **museum** of the history of the artisan in the Nizhny Novgorod region. The entrance is however somewhat hidden on the right hand side of the building in the side entrance. At the end of the Bolshaya Pokrovskaya is the cinema Oktyabr', with its small forecourt. It is the largest cinema in the city center.

Along the entire Bolshaya Pokrovskaya are metal figures, which are great for photographs, especially the goat opposite the Drama Theater, which is popular with children.

CHKALOV MONUMENT AND STAIRCASE

The monument of the pilot Valery Chkalov (1904-1938) was erected two years after his tragic death during a test flight. It was created by the sculptor Isaak Mendeleevich (1887-1952). Chkalov was a test pilot, and his record flight from Moscow to Portland (Oregon, USA) over the North Pole in 63.5 hours made him famous. On the marble base, the flights are immortalized. His birthplace today bears his name – Chkalovsk – and is located about 100km from Nizhny up the Volga river. The monument is a popular meeting place to enjoy the sunset over the Strelka.

Directly behind the monument is the **Chkalov Staircase** (Чкаловская лестница). This is the connection from the upper to the lower Volga road. It was built between 1943-1949 by German prisoners of war to commemorate the Battle of Stalingrad. In 2013, both the staircase and the **Lower Volga Embankment** (Нижне-Волжская набережная) were completely renovated, and invite you to go for a walk or a bike ride. Unfortunately, the waterfront has only been renovated up to the Rechnoy Vokzal. Behind it is an "eternal construction site". At the lower end of the stairs, the **war ship "Geroy"** (hero), which was used in the Second World War and is now a monument. In 2014, a new statue in the form of a **stag**, the city's heraldic animal, was erected on the promenade along the city. It was donated by the Polish consulate to commemorate Polish-Russian friendship. The Chkalov Staircase is located in **Alexandrovsky Park** (see "Parks and Lakes" below).

FEDOROVSKY EMBANKMENT

The Fedorovsky Embankment (набережная Федоровского) –

named after the mineralogist Nikolay Fedorovsky (1886-1956) – invites you to stroll and linger. It is located above the **Roshdestvenskaya** street along the Oka. From here you have a nice view of the strelka (the headland between the Oka and the Volga), the suburbs, and especially the **Alexander Nevsky Cathedral**, both during the day and at night. In the summer, various open-air events take place here –for example salsa courses.

The pedestrian bridge is particularly popular with bridal couples, who can attach a lock to symbolize their everlasting covenant. In the vicinity of the

pedestrian bridge stands

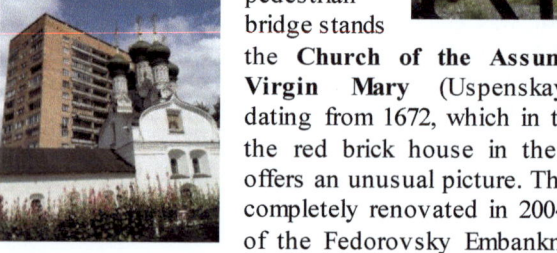

the **Church of the Assumption of the Virgin Mary** (Uspenskaya Tserkov) dating from 1672, which in the context of the red brick house in the background, offers an unusual picture. The church was completely renovated in 2004. At the end of the Fedorovsky Embankment you can see the vast expanse of Russia together with the life-size **Gorky monument**.

GORKY SQUARE

At the end of the pedestrian zone of the Bolshaya Pokrovskaya there is a large roundabout, in the center of which is a small park with the **Gorky monument** from 1939. The monument of Vera Ignatevna Muchina won the Allunion contest in 1939, but was only opened in 1953 due to the Second World War. All the important streets of the surrounding districts come together at this spot, and Gorky can be seen from afar with his weary coat. The spot is particularly popular with teenagers because of the McDonald's branch. Not far from the McDonald's is the large Rostelekom headquarters. About 500 meters further from Gorky Square, is the last large roundabout of the city center, Ploshad' Lyadova, which marked the city boundary until the 19th century.

KREMLIN

The Kremlin of Nizhny is the second largest in the country after the Moscow Kremlin. Its origins date back to the 14th century. However, construction work was only completed in 1511, with it continuing to undergo many changes over the centuries. It is surrounded by a red brick wall, about 2km long, studded with 13 towers. Five of the towers are square, the rest are round. The **Dmitry Tower**, the largest and considered the landmark of the

city, is located directly on Minin Square. It was from here that the construction of the Kremlin began, and it originally served as a defense center of the upper part of the city. The top of the

Dmitry Tower is crowned by a golden coat of arms – the stag. The Kremlin once served to protect against hostile attacks. It lost this function in the middle of the 17th century. Since the first half of the 19th century, the terrain of the Kremlin has changed considerably. Private houses were demolished and public buildings were erected in their place. During the Soviet period, the area experienced no less drastic changes. Instead of churches, administrative buildings were erected, so that the Kremlin lost its importance as a spiritual center. From 1949, the Kremlin was completely restored and retained its original appearance. Today, the Kremlin is the administrative center of the city and the region (Oblast). It is the seat of the city administration, the City Duma (parliament), the governing body (governor), the legislature of the oblast and the representative of the President of the Russian Federation in the Volga region. On the other hand, it is also the cultural center of Nizhny. Here you will find museums, exhibition rooms and the **Philharmonic** (further information in the section "Museums, Art and Culture"). Above all, however, the Kremlin is used by the locals to take a walk and take in the breathtaking view of the Volga. The area has several entrances and is open from 6 am to 10 pm in spring and summer (1 May - 31 October) and 6 am to 9 pm in autumn and winter (1 November - 30 April).

© http://www.ngiamz.ru/novosti/105-ob-yavleniya/219-polozhenie-o-poryadke-poseshcheniya-nizhegorodskogo-kremlya.html

ETERNAL FLAME

As in any major Russian city, there is also an eternal flame in Nizhny in memory of the fallen soldiers of the Second World War. It is customary for newly-wed bridal couples to put flowers on the eternal flame on their wedding day. In addition, the cadet pupils  regularly hold an honorary guard ceremony there.

KREMLIN WALL

The Kremlin wall which we see today does not correspond to the original, because it has been restored and rebuilt over the decades. The latest renovation was completed in 2013 with the Zachatskaya Tower. Various segments of the Kremlin wall can be explored by walking along it. A total of about 2/3 of the entire wall is accessible. The entrance to the wall is directly behind the passage of the Dimtry Tower. Going up the stairs, you will find the ticket office on the right-hand side. The walk is open from May to November. It is recommended to return along the outside wall. Arriving at the **Zachatkaya Tower**, you will be able to visit the museum, where you will find the first foundation wall and a photo exhibition about the progress of the construction work.

Opening hours: from May to November daily 10 am - 10 pm (Monday closed)

MICHAEL THE ARCHANGEL CATHEDRAL

In the center of the Kremlin is the Michael the Archangel Cathedral (Собор Михаила Архангела). It was built in 1631 to commemorate the victory of the people led by Minin and Pozharsky over the Poles. The site has had a church on it since the city was founded. In 1962 the body of Kozma Minin was moved here, as the original church where the tomb had previously been, was demolished.

The government buildings to the right and left of the Cathedral were built towards the end of the 18th century.

MININ AND POZHARSKY SQUARE

The Minin and Pozharsky Square (площадь Минина и Пожарского) is the central square of the city. It is, on the one side, surrounded by stately houses, which reflect the historical wealth of the city. On the other side, it is bordered by the Kremlin wall. From here, the Chkalov staircase leads down to the Volga Embankment. During festivals the plaza is closed to traffic and becomes a stage as stalls are erected. Particularly at the end of the year, a big Christmas tree is a real sight.

On entering the square from the street leading to the Volga river, the new splendor of the **former city parliament (Duma),** renovated in 2014, radiates immediately. It sits directly on the corner of **Bolshaya Pokrovskaya** and the square. It was built from 1899-1904 on behalf of the merchant N. Bugrov, who then gave it to the city. Since 2014, the court of the Nizhny Novgorod region has been located there.

Across the street is a small park with fountains. It is illuminated during summer evenings. The town's first water supply system was built here in 1847.

Directly opposite the **Dmitry Tower**, in a small park, is the **Minin Monument**. It dates back to the 1930s.

Minin Square is lined with other impressive buildings, along a line from the Minin Monument to the banks of the Volga River. The first corner building is today's **Gymnasium No. 1** which offers extended German lessons (the inscription on the door is also in German). Students here can take an exam and study for the German language diploma, which entitles them to study at a German university. To the right, in a building of the Lobachevsky University, there is a small, hidden **Pushkin Museum**. Going down from the Minin Square towards the Volga is a **former Priest's Seminary**. It dates from 1827 and houses the **Minin University**. Particularly striking are the eight white columns in the entrance area. Next to the building is a small square, in the middle of which is another **bust of Minin**, surrounded by a flower bed.

A final assemblage of buildings lies further down the Minin Street. The green-coloured building of the former shipping company "Volga" is situated on the corner of the Verkhnevolzhskaya Naberezhnaya (the Upper Volga Embankment). It was built at the beginning of the 20th century. Again, the pillars, especially the rondel, are noteworthy. Today, the administration of the **Medical Academy** is located here.

PECHERSKY ASCENSION MONASTERY

The Pechersky Ascension Men's Monastery (Вознесенский Печерский Мужской Монастырь) is situated on the banks of the Volga river in the direction of Kazan. The founding of the monastery goes back to the 14th century. However, it was completely destroyed by a landslide around 1600 and rebuilt 30 years later, about 2km away, where it stands today. The entire complex is surrounded by a predominantly white stone wall with round, corner towers. The towers are topped with a weather vane in the shape of an angel. At the center is the Ascension Cathedral. The four-cornered tower beside the clock is the bell tower. Along the Monastery walls one can easily recognize the Bishop's chambers, the monk's cells, a hospital, and the Peter-Paul's church at the far end. There are also two other churches on the site: the Church of Yefimy Suzdalsky just before the entrance in front of the Cathedral, and the Church of the Assumption at the other end of the Cathedral. Both are quite

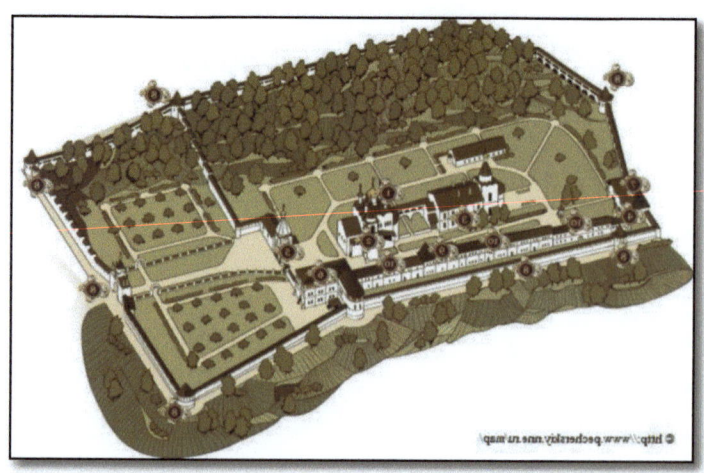

© http:\\www.pechersky.nne.ru\map

simple. A dining room extends between the Cathedral and the Church of the Assumption. The main gate, today's access to the site, was added in the 19th century.

http://www.pecherskiy.nne.ru/

ROZHDESTVENSKAYA STREET

The Rozhdestvenskaya (Рождественская улица) is one of the oldest streets of the city, and is located in the lower part of the center of Nizhny, parallel to the Lower Bank Street (Nizhne-Volzhskaya Naberezhnaya / Нижне-Волжская набережная). Here one can admire very beautiful, old houses with many details and decorations, built by wealthy merchant families. Many buildings date back to the 19th century and used to be banks, shops and residential buildings. In 2013, the road was completely renovated and today invites you to stroll on and visit a lot of different restaurant.

At the beginning of the street, where today the French restaurant Gavrosh (Гаврош) is located, was the **Rukavishnikov-Bank** (no.23). It was built based on the design by a Russian architect Fyodor Shekhtel from 1908-1916. Pay attention to the sculptures of the worker and the peasant woman beside the information sign, which symbolize industry on the one hand and agriculture on the other. It is a gigantic complex whose size can only be guaged from the Lower Volga Embankment (Нижне-Волжская Набережная), with its imposing façade in gothic style.

In the middle of the street you will find **Markin Square** (пл. Маркина), containing a small park with a fountain and a **memorial** to the heroes of the Volga war fleet. The park is

bounded on the Volga River by the **River-boat Station** (Rechnoy Vokzal - Речной вокзал), and by a former **gallery** owned by the merchants Blinov on the side of Rozhdestvenskaya street. The large brick building with the striking corner tower dates back to the 1870s and used to house hotels, restaurants and shops. The River-boat Station dates to 1964 and looks like a ship. Boat trips and river excursions can be taken from here (see "Recreation and Sports" below).

Walking along the street, you will find the most extraordinary church in the city – the **Cathedral of the Blessed Virgin Mary** (Церковь Собора Пресвятой Богородицы). It is unique in various ways – the red color and the brilliant towers, but also the so-called Stroganov style, a play of the Russian baroque style. It was built in 1719 on behalf of the Stroganov family. The Stroganovs were a powerful merchant dynasty, becoming rich in the salt trade. They had a mansion and an estate not far from the church. The property (no. 43-45) in classicist  style, consists of a house, two adjoining buildings, and a courtyard which was open to the river at that time.

There is a specific travel guide app for the street (*http://nn-guide.ru/*). You will find a QR code for scanning on your smartphone at various buildings. Very informative and very well done, but unfortunately available only in Russian.

SAINT JOHN THE BAPTIST CHURCH

The church in honor of the birth of John the Baptist (Храм Рождества Иоанна Предтечи) is picturesquely situated below the Kremlin wall near the Ivanov tower at the beginning of the **Rozhdestvenskaya street**. It was built in 1683. At this time there were already wooden churches, which, however, burnt down. The location was formerly strategic, as the main entrance to the Kremlin was at the Ivanov Tower. In the Soviet period the church was largely destroyed and unused. However, it was completely renovated in 2005 and now shines in new splendor.

The large square in front of St. John's Church is the "place of the people's unity" (площадь Народного Единства) and the location of the **Minin and Pozharsky memorial**. The monument was designed by Ivan Martos (1754-1835) and commemorates the popular uprising of 1612. Kosma Minin called on the citizens of Nizhny to defend themselves against the

invading Poles. The version of the memorial in Nizhny is actually a copy. The original has been on Moscow's Red Square since 1818. The famous painting on the great wall of Konstantin Makovsky (1839-1915) "Minin," can be viewed in the **art museum** on the Verkhnnevolzhskaya Naberezhnaya, 3/ the Upper Volga Embankment, 3 (see under "Museums, Art and Culture - Art Museum"). In 2005 the 4th of November was set as a public holiday to celebrate The Day of Unity of the People (see "Holidays and celebrations").

TRADE FAIR

Situated directly on the Oka River, the Nizhegorodskaya Yarmarka (Нижегородская Ярмарка) is one of the city's major buildings. After the fire of the old fairground in Makaryev (see below "excursion destinations - Makaryev-monastery") the fair was moved from Markayev to Nizhny in the early 19th century. Nizhny was described as the gateway between Asia and Europe, as it was Russia's largest exhibition center in the 19th century. This changed only after the construction of the railway from Moscow to Siberia. There were no fairs at the time of the Soviet Union, since Nizhny was a closed city for foreigners. The central red building, as can be seen today, was built in the late 19th century. It is externally elaborate with white stucco and is illuminated beautifully at night. The ground floor is open daily between 10 am and 7 pm and houses small shops. On the back of the fair is the entrance to the *Museum of the Sciences* "Kwarki" (see below "Traveling with Children"). On the first floor is the beautiful chamber of coat of arms, which is however only accessible during special events. The **new trade fair building** on the right was built between 1993-1996. Today, the site is used not only for trade fairs, but also for concerts, congresses and exhibitions.

http://www.yarmarka.ru/

The **Cathedral of the Savior** (Спасский Собор / Spassky Sobor) is within walking distance along the three parallel streets behind the exhibition. It was built between 1817 and 1822, and it was therefore also built during the time when the trade fair moved from Makaryev to Nizhny.

VERKHNEVOLZHSKAYA NABEREZHNAYA

The Upper Volga Embankment (Verkhnevolzhskaya Naberezhnya/Верхне-Волжская набережная) is one of the main tourist attractions in Nizhny, with a beautiful view of the Volga and the expanse of Russia. Be like the locals and just stroll along the street in the evenings.

At the beginning of the street (near the Kremlin) there are some interesting museums. Immediately after the administration building of the **Medical Academy** (see above "Minin and Pozharsky Square") stands the **House of Architects** (Дом Архитектора). There are changing exhibitions and occasional concerts. A little further, after the former hotel ("Volzhsky Otkos") Rossiya, follows the **Art Museum**. Directly opposite (erected in 2014) is a 2m high bust of Dmitry Sirotkin, the city mayor from 1913-1917.

Probably the most beautiful building on both the street and in the town is the former **Rukavishnikovs' Estate** (Усадьба Рукавишниковых), now a museum and venue for concerts (see "Museums, Art  and Culture"). **Sergey M. Rukavishnikov** (1852-1914) was a merchant and industrialist from Nizhny. The house is designed, both inside and out, in a sumptuous and elaborate Italian style, and reflects the wealth of the family dynasty. At the end of the 19th century it was by far the most expensive house ever built in Nizhny, and it was one of the first to have electricity and an elevator. If you want to continue walking in the footsteps of the Rukavishnikovs, a trip by car to the summer residence, which is just 1.5 hours outside of Nizhny (see below "excursions") is recommended.

About 100m further stands – in the absolute structural contrast to the Rukavishnikovs' Estate, and built 100 years after it – the **Hotel Oktyabrskaya** (Гостиница Октябрьская). In front of it is a small square with a **monument** in honor of Pyotr Nesterov (1887-1914). Nesterov was born in Nizhny. He was known as a pilot who flew a loop for the first time. He died in World War I during a mission. On the opposite side of the street is a miniature plane as seen at the beginning of the 20th century. At the other end of the square, on Minin Street, there is a beautiful little church – Church of the Icon of the Mother of God "Joy of All who Sorrow" (Церковь Иконы Божией Матери "Всех Скорбящих Радость").

Continue along the street and explore the architecture of the early 20th century, as well as the historical wealth of the city. This was where the elites used to live. The large red complex with the striking white sculptures is the **Technical University**. Below the waterfront on the slope there is the **Alexandrovsky Garden** (Alexandrovsky Sad / Александровский сад) (see "Parks and Lakes" below).

Parks and Lakes

Nizhny Novgorod is a comparatively green city with many parks. Especially in the center, there are many green oases where you can go for a walk or relax on a bench. There is a playground in almost every park.

ALEXANDROVSKY SAD

The Alexandrovsky Garden was the first public park in Nizhny. It lies on a hillside between the upper and lower Volga River (Верхне- и Нижне-Волжская набережная), not far from the Kremlin, and is about 35 ha. It was commissioned by Tsar Nicholas I in the 1830s. He ordered all the buildings on this site demolished and laid out a park in the English landscape style. Nicholas I. dedicated the garden to his wife Alexandra, which is the name given to the park. After the Second World War, the **Chkalov Stairs** (see above "Sights") were built and integrated into the park. In the summer, it offers shade due to the large, old trees, as well as concerts or open-air cinema. In winter, the locals cross-country ski on self-prepared runs. It is the ideal place to relax in the center of the city with a beautiful view of the vastness of Russia and the Volga river. You can easily forget that you are in the middle of a big city. At the end of the park, you will find a hotel that bears the same name (see "Hotels & Accommodation" below).

BOTANICAL GARDEN

The Botanical Garden is part of Lobachevsky University and was founded in 1934 on the initiative of Professor Sergey Stankov (1892-1962). Professor Stankov was also its first director. The complex is 35 ha in size and is located in the south-east of the city, not far from the Gagarina Avenue on Botanitshesky Sad road. There is also a greenhouse with tropical plants. A visit to the botanical garden is only possible after prior registration from May to October and only with a guided tour.

Opening hours: Monday-Friday 9 am-5pm; Closed on weekends

Address: Botanichesky Sad Street 1 (ул. Ботанический сад, д.1)

Phone: 8 (831) 465-51-41

http://www.unn.ru/botanicus/

KULIBIN PARK

This park, which was named after **Ivan Kulibin** (1735-1818), is located between Maxim Gorky Street and Belinskogo Street, right next to the Youth Theater (see "Traveling with Children"). It covers 12 ha. Not far from the youth theater, is a **bust of Kulibin**. He was born in Nizhny, and was a mechanic, watchmaker and inventor. At the other end of the park stands the **Church of St. Apostles Peter and Paul** (Храм Святых Апостолов Петра и Павла). Here is also **Kulibin´s grave** with a memorial plaque. This can be explained by the fact that a graveyard was located on the present park site from 1775-1940. This, however, is the only reference to its earlier life. In the 1960s, the church was transformed into a cinema, and was rededicated to its original purpose only in 1990.

MESHERSKOYE LAKE

Mesherskoye Lake (Мещерское Озеро) is about 1km long, making it the largest lake in the city. Locals swim there. It is located in the suburbs near the shopping center Sed'moe Nebo. On the side of Meshersky Boulevard there is a small sand beach for sunbathing. There are two pedestrian bridges across the lake and you can take a nice walk. However, you can also see the garbage, which is washed to the shore, which is not exactly inviting to go for a swim.

PUSHKIN PARK

Pushkin Park is also located at Belinskogo Street (улица Белинского), a little past Gorky Square. This is a small birch park surrounded by high-rise buildings with a modern playground. At the edge of the park is a large aerial. A new opera house was to be built in the park, but met great resistance from the residents.

SHYOLKOVSKY HUTOR

The urban forest (Щёлковский хутор) is the largest park in the city. Because of its three lakes it is popular in the summer, especially for swimming or sunbathing on the small sandy beach. Many families or young people also use the park for grilling. Inquire beforehand, however, if open fires are allowed (in the summer months the fire risk is high, so that grilling in the park is often forbidden). Unfortunately, environmental awareness has not yet developed so that garbage is often simply left behind. In winter, it is the most beautiful place for cross-country skiing. In the immediate vicinity of the park is a ski rental (see below "Recreation & Sports"). Unlike in the other parks, tracks are prepared through the forest or you simply walk over the frozen lakes. At the entrance of the park is homonymous architecture and a local museum (see "Museums, art and culture").

SORMOVSKY PARK

As the name suggests, the park is located in the Sormovo region, in the direction of Moscow. It is primarily a leisure park with many attractions for the young and old – an all-season ice skating rink, zoo, fun fair with various children's and adults' rides, a ferris wheel, a go-kart track and an outdoor swimming pool (see below "travelling with children"). There are two guarded parking spaces (80 rubles per day) on the Engels Street (улица Энгельса). The fee-based park attractions can not be paid for in cash, so a card for 50 rubles must be purchased at the cash desk. But you should not compare the to the European standards for an amusement park, so as not to be disappointed. It is mostly noisy and there are only few rides. If you leave the attractions behind, you can have a nice walk in the summer in the extensive park. Part of the park is also a lake. There is even a small sandy beach and a nice cafe with a terrace overlooking the water.

If you would like to have some barbecue, you can also rent a **barbecue place** and equipment in a closed area within the park on a small lake for 4000 rubles per day.

http://sormovopark.ru/

SWITZERLAND RECREATION PARK

Switzerland Park is the second largest, and one of the most famous parks in Nizhny. Its origins date back to the beginning of the 20th century. It is located in the upper part of the city, between the Gagarina Avenue

and the high bank of the Oka river, from where you have a nice view of the lower part of the city. With a length of 3.5 km it invites you for walking and relaxation. The entrance to the park is free. The first stop from the city is Tobolskiye Kazarmi (Тобольские Казармы), and the last stop is Myza (Мыза). If you

get off at the Cinema Elektron (кинотеатр Электрон) stop, you will come directly to the **Monument** dedicated to the soldiers from Nizhny who died in Afghanistan and Chechnya. In the summer the **fun fair** is interesting for children as well as adults (daily from 10 a.m. to 8 p.m.). It offers many rides – a ferris wheel (entrance from Meditsinskaya Street), carousel, carscooter (entrance from Surikova Street). Food is also available, and in particular the Shashliks are recommended. In winter, the park is ideal for cross-country skiing. There is even a small slope below the park for downhill skiing (see below "Recreation & Sports").

Museums, Art and Culture

Nizhny has great cultural offerings. You can enjoy them more if you understand Russian, but even without any knowledge of the language, the city offers something for every taste. When visiting a museum, note that ticket sales end about 30 minutes before closing. Each spring there is a "night of museums", where all exhibits can be visited free of charge and some special guided tours are offered.

ARSENAL

The Arsenal houses the Museum of Modern Art and is located in the Kremlin (Corpus 6) along the Kremlin wall. It was extensively renovated. In 2015, the second part was completed and reopened. The Museum houses temporary exhibitions and a small café. The Arsenal can also be rented for events. Concerts are held occasionally. It is simple and spacious, and the walls are unplastered so that the brick is visible, which gives it a very special ambience.

Opened daily from 12am to 8pm (except Mondays).

http://www.ncca.ru/nnovgorod

ART MUSEUM

The Art Museum comprises over 10,000 exhibits and is divided into two buildings. Exhibits of the Russian art are in the Kremlin (Corpus 3). The most important Western European art is located on Verkhnevolzhskaya Street 3. There you should definitely look at the room-high painting (7mx6m) by the Russian painter Konstantin Makovsky (1839-1915) "The Call of Minin" (1896). The piece took six years to complete. Since 1972 it has been admired in the specially designed room in the museum. This room is somewhat hidden. Walk past the wardrobe to the second floor. (For more information on Minin, see "Sights – St. John the Baptist Church".)

Opening hours: daily 11 am - 6 pm

Thursday 12 - 8pm

Closed on Tuesdays

http://www.artmuseumnn.ru/

http://www.artmuseumnn.ru/kartina-k-e-makovskogo-vozzvanie-minina/

CAR MUSEUM

Museum of the GAZ-plant. Old cars, especially the well-known Volga. Approx. 30 vehicles and history of the car industry and the GAZ plant. The museum is easy to reach by metro.

Opening hours:	Monday-Thursday 9 am-6pm
	Friday 9 am-5pm
	Saturday 9 am-4pm
Address:	Lenin Avenue 95 (not far from the station Komsomolskaya Prokhodnaya / Комсомольская проходная)
Telephone:	(831) 290-86-98 (Guided tours need to be pre-ordered)

http://xn----8sbigjekv7d.xn--p1ai/

COMEDY THEATER

The Comedy Theater is also close to Bolshaya Pokrovskaya. Program and tickets are available at the ticket office and on the website.

Address: Gruzinskaya Street 23 (ул. Грузинская, 23)

http://www.comedia.nnov.ru/

CONSERVATORY

The academy of music trains the musicians of tomorrow. The entrance is somewhat hidden. When you are at Piskunova street, in front of the posters of the pre-announcements, walk along the narrow alley at the park. You will come across the building shortly. Regular concerts are held not only by students. Current events can be viewed on the website. The highlight is, however, the **Alexander Schuke organ** from Potsdam from the year 1960. You should not miss an organ concert with this beautiful instrument.

Address: Piskunova Street 40 (ул. Пискунова, 40)

http://www.nnovcons.ru/

DOBROLUBOV LITERARY MEMORIAL MUSEUM

In the former residential house of Nikolay Dobrolubov (1836-1861) a museum about the literary scholar is installed. It is somewhat hidden near the Bolshaya Pokrovskaya. As the tramway crosses the pedestrian zone, a small one-way street leads directly to the museum behind the popular photo-motif of the metal sculpture of a couple. You must first buy a ticket in the large building next to the former house.

Address: Lykovaya Damba 2 (ул. Лыковая Дамба 2)

Entrance fee: foreigners pay 150 Rubel

Opening hours: 9 am-5pm daily

http://www.dobrolyubov-museum.ru/

DRAMA THEATER

One of the most beautiful buildings on the Bolshaya Pokrovskaya is the Drama Theater (see the photo above under "Sights"). It is named after Maxim Gorky. The current program is available on the website. Tickets can be purchased directly with a credit card online.

Address: Bolshaya Pokrovskaya 13 (ул. Большая Покровская, 13)

http://www.drama.nnov.ru/

EXHIBITION HALL

Right at the beginning of the Bolshaya Pokrovskaya, on the left, there is a picture gallery spread over several floors with different exhibitions. Highly recommended is the second floor, with pictures made of leaves by Alexander Yurkov (Александр Юрков – 1935-2014) in the exhibition of leaves (выставка листьев). Looking at the pictures, it is hard to believe that the artist did not use any painting but only dried leaves and glue.

Monday closed; Otherwise open from 12am to 7pm; Entrance fee 100 rubles.

LIBRARY

The municipal library is within walking distance of the Kremlin, at the beginning of Varvarskaya Street. You need a membership card to borrow books (request at the library). Since 1999, thanks to the Goethe-Institut, there has been a German reading room with exclusively German-language literature. German films are shown and discussed at regular intervals. Information can be found on the VKontakte page.

Address: Varvarskaya Street 3 (ул. Варварская, 3)

Opening hours: Monday - Thursday 9am - 8pm

                 Friday - Saturday 10am-6pm

https://vk.com/dsaal_nn

http://www.nounb.sci-nnov.ru

RIVER FLEET MUSEUM

The River Fleet Museum (Muzey Retshnogo Flota) is located in the center of the city, not far from the Kremlin, on the 4th floor of the Academy of Shipping. If you are interested in model ships, you should pay a visit. At the main entrance, you first have to submit a document to get in.

Opening hours: weekdays 9am-4pm

Entrance fee: 100 rubles

Address: Minin street 7 (ул. Минина, дом 7)

http://www.vsawt.ru/newsite/departments/museum/

MAXIM GORKY MUSEUMS

What many do not know is that the name "Maxim Gorky" was only the artist's pseudonym. His real name was Alexey Maksimovich Peshkov (1868-1936). Gorky means "bitter" in Russian. Nizhny Novgorod was from 1932-1990 named Gorky in memory of the writer born here. To this day, one cannot avoid Gorky in Nizhny Novgorod. There are monuments and three museums named after him, as well as many other public places.

KASHIRIN HOUSE

The house, where Gorky lived as a child for a short time, was transformed into a museum in 1938. This house accommodated 16 people at various times. Gorky lived here at the age of 3-4 years with his mother with his grandfather's family after his father died of cholera. The museum displays items of crafts and everyday life from the 19th century. You can read the autobiographical novel "My Childhood" (1913) as an inspiration.

Address: Pochtovy Syezd 21 (Почтовый съезд, 21)

Opening hours: 9am-5pm daily

Thursday 11am-6pm

Tuesday and Wednesday closed

http://www.museums.unn.ru/danco/expos/kh.shtml

LITERATURE MUSEUM

The building, which has housed the Literary Museum since 1934, used to be a town house. Unfortunately, the house is in dire need of renovation. Nevertheless, a visit is worthwhile, if only for the interior decoration. The richly decorated and stately rooms with stucco, wood and marble staircase give an insight into the life of the upper classes at the end of the 19th century. The museum is primarily concerned with presenting the diversity of the writer's connections with Nizhny while telling stories about events and people.

Address: Minin Street 26 (ул. Минина, 26)

Opening hours: 9am-5pm daily

Thursday 11pm-7pm

Monday and Tuesday closed

http://www.museums.unn.ru/danco/expos/lm.shtml

RESIDENTIAL HOUSE

In this house, Gorky and his family rented an apartment from 1902-1904. This was also his last apartment before he left Nizhny Novgorod. During his time here, he wrote 50 pieces. The museum was opened in 1971. It shows the life of the family, but also the relationships with contemporaries and like-minded people. It is said that the apartment was the center of the social, cultural and artistic life of the city.

Address: Semashko Street 19 (ул. Семашко, 19)

Opening hours: 9am-5pm daily

Wednesday 11am-7pm

Monday and Thursday closed

http://www.museums.unn.ru/danco/expos/hm.shtml

MUSEUM OF HANDICRAFTS

The Museum of the History of Arts and Crafts of Nizhny Novgorod is located in the center of the pedestrian zone (Bolshaya Pokrovskaya) on the 4th floor above the big souvenir shop. The entrance is somewhat hidden. It is on the right-hand side of the souvenir shop after the passage between the souvenir shop and the Puppet Theater. A visit to the lovingly furnished museum is worthwhile, however. Wooden carvings, icons, toys and everything that has been produced in the region and still produced today can be found here. If you do not have time to visit the museum, a virtual tour is possible on the website.

Address:	Bolshaya Pokrovskaya 43 (ул. Большая Покровская, 43)

Opening hours: daily 10am-5pm (Monday closed)

http://www.ngiamz.ru/filialy/muzej-istorii-khudozhestvennykh-promyslov.html

OPERA AND BALLET THEATER

The opera and ballet theater is named after A. S. Pushkin (Театр оперы и балета имени Пушкина). For this reason, in front of the building, which was built in 1903, is a bust of Pushkin. A varied program is offered. Tickets can be purchased directly on the website. The public transport stop of the same name is located directly in front of the door.

Address:	Belinskogo Street 59/2 (улица Белинского, 59/2)

http://operann.ru/

PARK POBEDY

For those who find that the exhibition of the war equipment in the Kremlin is not enough, there are more tanks in the Park of Victory in memory of the Second World War.

Address:	Naberezhnaya Grebnogo Kanala (набережная Гребного канала)

http://park-pobeda-nnov.ru/

PHILHARMONIC

The Philharmonic is not far from the Eternal Flame in the Kremlin. There is also a ticket office. Individual tickets can be purchased on the website, subscriptions only at the checkout. The concert offerings are varied and at a high level. The concert season starts in September. Concert subscriptions are popular, for example the series "5 out of 10". Five concerts at a price of 2000 rubles – this is only available in Russia. During the summer break, the orchestra plays every Friday afternoon for free. However, you should be there in time if you want to get a seat.

http://music-nn.ru/

PHOTOGRAPHY-MUSEUM

In a side street, not far from the Bolshaya Pokrovskaya and the Drama Theater, the Photography Museum is quite inconspicuous on Piskunova Street 9a. It was opened in 1992 and, over two floors, has displays on the history of photography and, which is perhaps even more interesting, old photographs of Nizhny Novgorod.

Entrance fee:	adults 150 Rubel
	Children / pensioners 75 Rubel
Opening hours:	Monday - Wednesday 11am - 7pm
	Thursday 12 - 8 pm
	Friday closed
	Saturday + Sunday 11am - 5pm
Address:	Piskunova Street 9a (ул.Пискунова, 9а)

http://www.fotomuseum.nnov.ru/

PLANETARIUM

Right next to the Circus, the Planetarium is located near the railway station on the Oka bank. It was opened in 1948 and moved into this building in 2005. The Planetarium has its own observatory. The program is available on the website. There is plenty to see for children. Tickets can only be purchased on site.

| Address: | Revolyutsionnaya Street 20 |
| | (ул. Революционная, 20) |

http://www.planetarium-nn.ru/

PUSHKIN MUSEUM

Pushkin visited Nizhny on September 2.-3. in 1833. This was reason enough to open a small museum. There are no more than a handful of exhibits spread out over two rooms. The entrance is somewhat hidden in the adjoining building of the Gymnasium No. 1 near the Minin square. Walk through the archway, and the door to the museum is on the right. Entrance costs 80 rubles. Open Tuesday to Saturday 10am-5pm.

Address: Minin square 4 (площадь Минина и Пожарского, 4)

RADIO LABORATORY

In the early 20th century, the first Russian radio valves and powerful radio transmitters were engineered here. Today you can learn about it in the museum. Admission 50 rubles; Weekdays 10 am-5pm.

Address: Vekhne-Volzhskaya Naberezhnaya 5 (Верхне-Волжская набережная, 5).

http://radiolaboratorija.ru/

RUKAVISHNIKOVS' ESTATE

The Rukavishnikovs' Estate (Усадьба Рукавишниковых) on Verkhnevolzhskaya Naberezhnaya 7 was once the home of the merchant Sergey Rukavishnikov (see above "sights"). Today it is used as a museum and as a venue for concerts.

Opening hours: Tuesday-Thursday 10am-5pm

Friday-Sunday and holidays from 12 to 7 pm

Monday and last Thursday every month closed

Address: Verkhne-Volzhskaya Naberezhnaya 7 (В.-Волжская наб., д.7)

http://www.ngiamz.ru/filialy/usadba-rukavishnikovykh.html

SAKHAROV MUSEUM

Andrey Dmitriyevich Sakharov (1921-1989) was a physicist who developed the Soviet hydrogen bomb and made important contributions to nuclear fusion, particle physics and cosmology. In 1939 he joined the Red Army. He was convinced that the nuclear balance of power between East and West ensured peace. For his achievements, he was awarded the Order of Stalin and the Hero of the Soviet Union, and at the age of 32 was the youngest member of the Soviet Academy of Sciences. From 1955, however, he became an opponent of nuclear weapons tests and of ever-growing nuclear rearmament. He called for the release of political prisoners, demanded the democratization of the Soviet Union, and condemned the defeat of the Prague Spring in 1968 and the invasion of the Red Army in Afghanistan in 1979. In 1968 he wrote the memorandum "Disarmament, Coexistence and Intellectual Freedom" for which he received the Nobel Peace Prize in 1975. He himself could not receive the Prize because he did not receive an exit permit. Instead his wife Elena Bonner went to Oslo. In 1980 he was banished to Nizhny Novgorod. In 1986, Gorbachyov lifted the ban. Sakharov went to Moscow, where he resumed his political activities. In 1989, he was elected to the Congress of People's Deputies. In a heated debate in Parliament, he so irritated the Soviet functionaries that the microphone was turned off. The next day he succumbed to a heart attack in his home. He died in December 1989 in Moscow.

The museum is located at Gagarin Avenue 214 (apartment 3), almost on the outskirts, not far from the bus stop "Музей Имени Сахарова" (Sakharov Museum) in a slab building settlement. The entrance to the Museum is on an inconspicuous, gloomy home entrance. The small bronze shield with the inscription "Museum Andrey Dmitryevich Sakharov", which is difficult to read from afar, can be easily overlooked. Pressing the "3" on the bell will sound a signal and the heavy iron door opens. Of special note is the apartment on the ground floor allocated by the KGB to Sakharov and his second wife Elena Georgievna Bonner. For those times it was above average with four small rooms, a kitchen, a balcony and a bathroom. After all, attention was paid to the merits and worldwide recognition of the exile. The rooms are still largely kept in their original condition, since the furniture belonged to the apartment. These relatively favorable housing conditions, however, were overshadowed by the monitoring of daily life and complete isolation from the outside world.

The museum is open daily from 10am to 5pm (Friday closed). Admission costs 70 rubles.

Address: Gagarin Avenue 214 (ул. Гагарина проспект, 214)

SHYOLKOVSKY HUTOR MUSEUM

The architecture and ethnographic museum (Архитектурно-этнографический музей Щёлковский хутор) is an open-air museum directly at the Shyolkovsky Hutor Park (see above "Parks and Lakes"). It shows a piece of the Russian history through its old wooden houses and churches. The museum has 14 exhibits, including two churches, residential buildings, barns, horse stables, as well as two mills. The exhibits were originals mainly from the Nizhny Novgorod region. Folklore events take place on special holidays.

Church on the roadside

It dates back to the end of the 17th century and is from the Gorodets region, it was brought to Nizhny in 1970. The church consists of three parts – the refectory, the main room and the altar, made of thick pine trunks.

Church on the hill

Built in 1731 in the Kstovo region and brought to Nizhny in 1975. The peculiarity is the multi-storey, octagonal tower.

Pavlov House

The house dates from the second half of the 18th century. It is from Rakovo and came to Nizhny in the 1980s. It is remarkable due to its carvings and interior furnishings.

Windmill and water mill

Built in the 19th century. The peculiarity of the windmill is the central column, which is firmly embedded in the ground. This meant that the entire mill turned into the wind direction.

Address:	Gorbatovskaya Street (ул. Горбатовская, д. 41 – Bus No. 28 terminal stop)
Entrance fee:	school children: 30 rubles, students / pensioners – 40 rubles, adults – 60 rubles
Opening hours:	15 November – 14 March: 10am-4pm
	15 March – 14 October: 10am-5pm

http://hutor-museum.ru/

SOLOISTS OF NIZHNY NOVGOROD

The chamber orchestra with 16 professional musicians was founded in 1990. There is no permanent conductor, but one of the soloists is also the musical leader. The concerts usually take place in special places, e.g., in the Planetarium or in the Rukavishnikovs' Estate.

http://www.solistynn.ru/

TECHNICAL MUSEUM

The museum, which has been created from a lifetime collection of a father and his son, shows everything that is old and has to do with technology. For this reason, the museum is also called "The Museum of Ancient Technology and Tools". The museum is located in the pedestrian zone above the large souvenir shop on the 3rd floor in the same building as the Museum of Handicrafts (see above). The entrance is slightly hidden on the right hand side of the building. The museum has only one large exhibition space, but most of the exhibits can be touched.

Opening hours:	Tuesday-Sunday 10am-6pm; Monday closed
Address:	Bolshaya Pokrovskaya 43 – 3rd floor (ул. Б. Покровская, д. 43, 3-ий этаж)
Entrance fee:	200 rubles

http://www.techmuzey.ru/

THEATER OF DRAMA SCHOOL

The theater, in which the actors-to-be perform, is located at the beginning of the pedestrian zone on the Bolshaya Pokrovskaya Street (Uchebny Teater/Учебный театр), seen from the Kremlin. The building with cats above the entrance is not to be missed. The students study at the drama school, which is located on Varvarskaya Street 3a (Нижегородское театральное училище им. Е.А. Евстигнеева - Варварская улица, 3а).

http://ntu-nn.ru/

TRAMWAY MUSEUM

The Tramway Museum (Музей трамваев) is one of the lesser-known museums due to its location on the outskirts. Six tramways and two trolley buses are shown. The oldest dates from the year 1896. It is especially interesting for children because the trams can be viewed not only from the outside, but also from the inside while still active tramways drive by to the adjoining large maintenance halls. However, only recommended in the summer, since in winter the snow is not cleared.

Opening hours: Mon-Fri 8am-12am and 12:30am-4:30pm Address: General Ivliyev Street (Generala Ivliyeva Street 1/ул. Генерала Ивлиева, 1) Trolleybus depot No.1

ZIFERBLAT

Actually, the Ziferblat is a café and therefore is out of place under this category – but on closer inspection, it is quite correct. The Ziferblat is a cozy apartment with very different rooms. You pay for the time you spend there. For the price paid, you can drink as much tea and coffee as you want. You can also bring your own food and warm it up in the microwave. There is always something happening. Music instruments are also available. In the evenings, there is a wide range of cultural activities – language groups, lectures, concerts, salsa dances and more. The idea came from Ivan Mitin. He founded the first Ziferblat in 2001 in Moscow. There are now ten of these cafes in Russia and even one in London. You can find out more about the latest cultural events on the VKontakte website. The apartment is not easy to find. It is located in a two-storey building behind the International Business Center (World Trade Center). In the window of the apartment you can see the logo from the outside – a mixture of a clock and a head. Walk through the entrance door and up the stairs to the first floor.

Address: Kovalikhinskaya Street 4a (ул. Ковалихинская, 4a)

https://vk.com/ziferblatnn

http://nino.ziferblat.net/en/

Cinema und Karaoke

Like any European city, Nizhny has modern cinemas. The problem with a visit to the cinema, however, is mostly the language. Most films are dubbed into Russian without subtitles. Sometimes an English film is shown in the original, but this is more of an exception.

7D CINEMA

In the middle of Bolshaya Pokrovskaya is a 7D cinema. You can experience 3D movies with additional special effects.

Address: Bolshaya Pokrovskaya Street 35a (Большая Покровская 35А)

http://4dkino-nn.ru/

FANTASTIKA

In the Fantastika shopping center there is a large cinema with 8 rooms (Cinema Park) showing current films. In addition, there are also 3D movies.

Address: Rodionova Street 187 B (ул. Родионова 187 B)

http://www.cinemapark.ru/multiplexes/show/13

ORLYONOK

The first cinema of the city was once in this building. Today it is a rather older cinema, but with its own charm. The repertoire is specially designed for children and adolescents.

Address: Bolshaya Pokrovskaya 39a (ул. Большая Покровская, 39a)

http://www.orlenok-kino.ru/

REKORD

The Rekord is an "alternative cinema". Current or mainstream films are not shown here. The cinema also offers no service and none of the comforts of a modern cinema.

Address: Piskunova Street 11/7 (ул. Пискунова, 11/7)

ROMANOV

This exclusive cinema is located on the 3rd floor of the luxury shopping center "Lobachevsky Plaza". The cinema hall even has double beds. Here you can also rent your own cinema room to watch the latest films, undisturbed on your own, or with your friends.

In addition, karaoke is offered (Sun-Wed from 6pm to 2am, Thurs-Sat from 6pm to 6am) and a possibility to rent a karaoke room.

Address: Alexeyevskaya Street 10/16 (ул. Алексеевская 10/16)

http://www.romanovnn.ru/

SED'MOYE NEBO

As in the Fantastika shopping center, there is also a cinema park in the Sed'moye Nebo shopping center. The cinema is the largest in the city with 10 theaters. It was opened in 2012 and has an IMAX.

Address: Betankura Street 1 (ул. Бетанкура д.1)

SPUTNIK

English-language films are available in the Kinoklub "Sputnik". This is a small cinema with about 20 seats and it is somewhat hidden in a backyard of the Bolshaya Pokrovskaya street. The cinema can also be rented for private showings. A ticket costs 100 rubles.

Address: Bolshaya Pokrovskaya 15b, Apartment 14 (ул.
                Б. Покровская дом 15-Б, к.14)

https://vk.com/sputnikinfo

http://www.sputniknn.narod.ru/

Dining & Drinking

There are many restaurants on the Bolshaya Pokrovskaya street as well as on the Rozhdestvenskaya street. It is impossible to list them all. Below is a small selection. Since May 2014 it is prohibited to smoke in restaurants. However, shisha is popular and permitted.

EXPENSIVE

BOCCONCHINO

A very good oven pizza is available at the Bocconchino. An excellent Italian restaurant with stylish ambience is located on the 3rd floor of the luxury shopping center Lobachevsky Plaza. A pizza costs between 370-900 rubles – a glass of wine just as much. From an order amount to 1600 rubles or above, there is a possibility of home delivery.

Address: Alexeyevskaya Street 10/16 (ул. Алексеевская, 10/16)

Opening hours: 12am-midnight

http://www.bocconcino.ru/en/

BOSS BAR

On the ground floor of the Lobachevsky Plaza there is a solid Boss Bar. The name may suggest something different, but it is more of a restaurant than a bar.

Address: Alexeyevskaya Street 10/16 (ул. Алексеевская, 10/16)

Opening hours: daily 12am-2am

http://www.bossbar.ru/

EXPEDITION

A visit to the restaurant Expedition is an absolutely extraordinary experience. The design is extraordinary, with a helicopter in the middle of the restaurant. As the name promises, the dishes are also adventurous: meat served from a tin can, or raw fish on an ice block. In any case, the kitchen will hold surprises for you. In summer the balcony offers a nice view of "the Strelka" (the confluence of the two main rivers the Volga and the Oka).

Address: Rozhdestvenskaya Street 1, below the Kremlin wall – (ул. Рождественская, 1/ул. Кожевенная, 16 б)

Opening hours: 12am-midnight

http://expedition-nn.ru/

MITRICH

This steakhouse is located in the International Business Center (World Trade Center). It has exceptionally good service. You can watch the cooks. Thought has also been given to children: there is a separate playroom with supervision.

Address: Kovalikhinskaya 8 (ул. Ковалихинская, 8, эт.2)

Opening hours: daily 11am-midnight

http://mitrichsteak.ru/

PYATKIN

Excellent Russian cuisine can be found in Pyatkin on Rozhdestvenskaya street. The restaurant belongs to the Pir group. There are eleven high-quality restaurants spread throughout Nizhny, each offering a particular cuisine. You can reserve a table on the website. **Traditional Russian dishes** you should try: Borsh (beet soup), Ukha (fish soup), Solyanka (meat soup), salad Olivé, salad Vinegret (beat salad), Selyodka-pod-Shuboy ("Herring under a fur coat", a herring and vegetable salad), ikra (caviar), blini (crepes), pelmeni (meat dumplings), pirozhky (stuffed pastries) and mors (mostly homemade juice from fruits).

Address: Rozhdestvenskaya Street 25 (Рождественская, 25)

Opening hours: 12am-midnight

http://pir.nnov.ru/pyatkin/

SPORTSBAR

The Sports Bar offers something for every taste. In the bar itself, sports are shown on large screens. You can enjoy a beer and a burger or a steak. In the summer, the adjacent beer garden has grilled dishes. The location of the restaurant is unbeatable. It is in the town center, yet quiet because it is nestled in a green park. It is therefore difficult to find on the first visit. On the first floor there is also a very cozy and stylish terrace in the summer.

Address: Piskunova Street 40 (ул. Пискунова, 40)

Opening hours: Monday-Thursday 8am-midnight

                Friday 8am-2am

                Saturday-Sunday 8am-2am

https://vk.com/sportbarnn

TIFFANI

By far the best location belongs to the restaurant "Tiffani" on the upper bank street, not far from the Kremlin. In an upscale atmosphere, you can enjoy extraordinary views of the Volga River. In the summer, the terrace is especially recommended. Late in the evening the restaurant changes into a bar.

Address: Verkhnevolzhskaya Naberezhnaya 8a (Верхне-Волжская наб., 8a)

http://tiffanibar.ru/

MEDIUM

ANGLIYSKOE POSOLSTVO

The "English Embassy" is a pub. For about 10 € you can get here a very good steak. On the first floor is a playroom for children, partly also with supervision. So you can relax and enjoy your meal.

Address: Zvezdinka Street 12 (ул. Звездинка, 12 – opposite the main post office)

Opening hours: Sunday-Thursday 8am-midnight

Friday-Saturday 8am-2am

http://pir.nnov.ru/englishpub/

BIBLIOTEKA

This restaurant is very popular with the locals. Mainly Italian cuisine with homemade pasta. You should book a table in advance. In the summer there is a small balcony to sit outside.

Address: Bolshaya Pokrovskaya Street 46, 2nd Floor (ул. Большая Покровская, 46, эт. 3)

Opening hours: daily 11am-10pm

http://www.biblioteca-nn.ru/

DRUZHKOVA KRUZHKA

A good Czech restaurant with rustic furniture right on the Bolshaya Pokrovskaya Street (Дружкова кружка). The Czech beer is especially recommended. Live bands regularly.

Address: Bolshaya Pokrovskaya Street 35 (ул. Большая Покровская, 35)

Opening hours: Friday-Saturday 12am-midnight

http://www.drkruzhka.ru/

HACHAPURI

In the restaurant "Hachapuri" (Хачапури) you can sample the cuisine of Georgia. It is particularly convenient that there is a picture of all the dishes on the menu, which makes the selection considerably easier. You should try "Hachapuri", which is freshly oven-baked bread with a cheese filling – quite greasy and filling. Otherwise the dishes with sheep meat are recommended.

Address: Rozhdestvenskaya Street 39 (ул. Рождественская, 39)

Opening hours: Sunday-Thursday 12am-midnight

Friday-Saturday 12am-2am

http://vhachapuri.ru/

IRISH PUB

Harat's is a chain that exists throughout Russia. As the name suggests, it's more like a pub than a restaurant. The menu is therefore limited. The facade of the house is notable.

Address: Varvarskaya Street 32 (ул. Варварская, 32)

http://www.harats.ru/

MOLOKO CAFE

Moloko means "milk" in Russian. This is a chain of nine restaurants in Nizhny. All the restaurants are unusual, exceptionally furnished, with attention to detail. The food is light and delicious. At the Moloko Café, on the first floor, there is also a nice veranda for a warm summer break.

Address: Alexeyevskaya Street 15 (ул. Алексеевская, 15)

Opening hours: Sunday-Thursday 12am-2am

Friday-Saturday 12am-6am

http://www.molokocafe.ru/

MOLOKO LETO

In the summer, the Moloko Leto (Молоко Лето) is an absolute insider tip. Overlooking the city's rooftops, you can relax in the cozy atmosphere with a cool drink on the terrace in the fresh air to escape the noise.

Address: Bolshaya Pokrovskaya Street 52 (ул. Большая Покровская, 52 – - in the shopping center "Lesnitsa" on the 3rd floor)

Opening hours: daily 12am-2am

MÜKKA

This cozy and distinctively furnished pizzeria was opened in 2015. It is part of the project "Food and Culture", which also includes the Moloko restaurants. The restaurant is situated in an old villa over three floors, each with a different atmosphere. In summer it is an absolute insider tip, because of the roof terrace. Pizzas are baked in a stone oven, but the portions are rather small.

Address: Osharskaya Street 36b (ул. Ошарская, 36Б)

Opening hours: Tuesday-Sunday 12am-11pm

http://mukkapizza.ru/

PLAKUCHAYA IVA

This restaurant „weeping willow" (Плакучая Ива) offers high quality Georgian cuisine. Meat dishes are recommended. The building looks like a small castle from the outside.

Address: Nizhnevolzhskaya   Naberezhnaya   23
                        (Нижневолжская наб., 23)

Opening hours: Sunday-Thursday 12am-midnight

                        Friday-Saturday 12am-2am

TANUKI

Sushi is very popular in Russia. For this reason, it is offered in many restaurants but also partly in supermarkets, with quite different quality. The general advice is, in restaurants which offer sushi as well as pizza and the Russian cuisine, be careful. The restaurant Tanuki is a beautifully decorated, thoroughly Japanese restaurant, with a large selection, good quality, and very good service.

Address: Maxim Gorky Square 5/76 (пл. Максима Горького, 5/76)

Opening hours: daily 11:30am-midnight

http://nn.tanuki.ru/

U ALEXANDRA

This restaurant is particularly recommended in the summer, as it is located on the Volga embankment and has a large outside area with comfortable booths. Unfortunately a very busy street runs directly along the restaurant. You should taste the freshly grilled meat (shashlik).

Address: Pechery Sloboda 112a (ул. Слобода Печёры, 112a)

Opening hours: daily 10am-1am

http://www.yalexandra-nn.ru/

VESYOLAYA KUMA

If you want to taste the Ukrainian cuisine, go to Vesyolaya Kuma. The restaurant is very comfortable. Particularly recommended are the Vareniki (stuffed dumplings) with cherries (Вареники с вишней) as a dessert. And of course the Borsh, which is originally from the Ukraine.

Address: Kostina Street 3 (ул. Костина, 3)

http://pir.nnov.ru/kuma/

LOW-COST

CHEF´S

Especially popular with students, since the food is cheap and freshly prepared. Sandwich, soup or salad for about 200 rubles. In a cozy, quiet atmosphere, you can even do homework quickly. There are two cafes. The café on Piskunova Street is larger and more comfortable.

Address: Minin Street 33 (Минина, 33)

Opening hours: Monday-Friday 8am-10pm

                       Saturday-Sunday 10am-10pm

Address:	Piskunova 24 (Пискунова, 24)
Opening hours:	Monday-Thursday 9am-11pm
	Friday 9am-midnight
	Saturday 10am-midnight
	Sunday 10am-11pm

http://chefscafe.ru/

MIRAYA

Miraya is a yoga center. However a small café is connected to it on the ground floor. The entrance is slightly hidden on the right hand sight of the building. The entrance door is decorated with two carved wooden piles. Between 1pm and 4pm, a business lunch is offered for 150 rubles.

Address: Alexeyevskaya Street 41 (ул. Алексеевская, д.41)

http://cafemiraya.ru/

SALUT BURGER

A project of a group of young people offering freshly made burgers. Very good and cheap. A burger costs 220 rubles. Not far from Bolshaya Pokrovskaya. Open daily from 12 noon. Mostly large crowds, which leads to longer waiting times.

Address: Oktyabrskaya Street 9a (ул. Октябрьская, 9А)

http://salutburgers.ru/

SHAURMA

Shaurma (Шаурма) means kebab. The best in the city is at the end of Belinskogo Street, near Lyadov Square. For this reason, there is always a long line. However, you can be sure that it is always fresh. Shaurma is freshly grilled meat from a charcoal barbecue with vegetables and mayonnaise wrapped in bread. For 140 rubles, it is better than any fast food.

Address: Kostina Street 13 (ул. Костина, 13)

http://shaurma-best.ru/

SOVOK

Noodle bar "Sovok" (Лапшичная "Совок") is very popular with young people. Pick the noodles and the ingredients, and the soup is freshly prepared before your eyes. Prepared quickly, it is cheap and tastes good.

Address: Bolshaya Pokrovskaya Street 2 (ул. Большая Покровская, 2)

Opening hours: daily 10am-10pm

https://vk.com/sowokfood

STOLLE

An absolute must-see is a visit to the self-service restaurant Stolle. Stolle is a chain that has existed since 2002 in many cities of Russia, and even in London and New York. The specialty is Russian cakes (Pirogy) of all types – from hearty to sweet. So the day can begin in a cozy atmosphere.

Address: Minin Square 2/2, entrance on the side of Alexeyevskaya Street (пл. Минина и Пожарского 2/2, вход с ул. Алексеевской)

Opening hours: 9am-9pm

Address: Ilyinskaya Street 98 (ул. Ильинская 98)

Opening hours: 9am-7pm

http://www.stolle.ru/

TIME FOR WINE

This wine bar is run by a young couple. They have a large wine selection, and you can order a bottle or a certain selection of wines per glass. The wines are offered at fair prices when compared to the usual wine prices in Russia. There are some small dishes to eat as well. Open daily from 4pm. However, somewhat difficult to find. It is in the middle of Bolshaya

Pokrovskaya Street, where the tram crosses the pedestrian zone next to the shopping center "Pokrovskiye Vorota".

Address: Bolshaya Pokrovskaya Street 20b (улица Большая Покровская, дом 20б)

http://timeforwine.ru/

FAST FOOD

The international fast food chains have also made it to Nizhny Novgorod. If you speak little Russian, this is very handy, because you know what there is on offer, and if in doubt, you can always view the pictures. The list below shows only the fast food chains, which are located in the city center. In every big shopping center there is, of course, a food court with a large offering.

Burger King

Bolshaya Pokrovskaya 42 (ул. Большая Покровская, 42)

daily 10am-10pm

http://burgerking.ru/ru/ru/index.html

KFC

Bolshaya Pokrovskaya 47 (ул. Большая Покровская, 47)

daily 10am-10pm

http://www.kfc.ru/restaurants/87

McDonalds

Gorky Square 2 (пл. Горького, 2)

daily 7am-11:30pm

http://www.mcdonalds.ru/

World of Pizza (Mir Pizzy)

Мир Пиццы (world of Pizza)

Bolshaya Pokrovskaya 4a (ул. Большая Покровская, 4a)

daily 11am-midnight

Minin Square 6 (пл. Минина и Пожарского, 6)

daily 11am-11pm

http://www.mirpizzy.com/

Starfood

Minin Street 16a (ул. Минина, 16a)

daily 9am-10pm

http://www.starfoodrf.ru/

CAFÉS

COFFEE CAKE

A cozy café. In the summer on Bolshaya Pokrovskaya Street there is also with a nice terrace to sit outside.

Opening hours: Monday-Thursday 8am-10pm

Friday-Sunday 24h

Address: Bolshaya Pokrovskaya Street 2 (ул. Большая Покровская, 2)

Rozhdestvenskaya Street 24 (ул.Рождественская 24)

www.coffee-cake.net

COFFEESHOP COMPANY

This café is a worldwide chain with 92 branches in Russia alone. In Nizhny, the location is directly at the beginning of the pedestrian zone and is open daily from 9am to 11pm.

Address: Bolshaya Pokrovskaya Street 2 (ул. Большая Покровская, 2)

www.coffeeshopcompany.ru

KONDITERSKAYA

The pastry shop has the French name "La Rochelle" (Ля Рошель) and is available in the town with six outlets. The menu ranges from cakes to pastries. There is also hot food, if you want to eat quickly. As a cozy café, it is not recommended. Better take a delicious piece of cake home with you. Cakes can also be ordered for birthdays or weddings. Open daily from 8am to 9pm.

Address: Bolshaya Pecherskaya Street 8 (ул. Б. Печерская, 8)

Bolshaya Pokrovskaya Street 30a (ул. Б. Покровская, 30 А)

Piskunova 18a (ул. Пискунова, 18 А)

Kostina 3 (ул. Костина, д. 3)

http://www.bigvolga.ru/

SHOKOLADNITSA

Shocoladnitsa is also a chain throughout Russia. Cozily furnished and directly opposite the Kremlin. Open daily from 10am to 10pm.

Address: Minin Square 11 (пл. Минина, 11)

Piskunova Street 8/8 (ул. Пискунова, 8/8)

www.shoko.ru

VOLKONSKY

This baker and confectioner is pricey, but worth it. You can get freshly baked baguette and other breads, and lots of tasty pastries. Pleasant ambience. Open daily from 7am.

Address: Piskunova Street 34 (ул. Пискунова, 34)

Dobrolyubova Street 9 (ул. Добролюбова, 9)

Semashko 30 (ул. Семашко, 30)

www.wolkonsky.com

OTHERS

DELIVERY SERVICE

If you do not want to go out to eat, food can also be delivered to your home comfortably via an App or the Internet. The site has a wide selection of restaurants, with something for everyone. Unfortunately, only available in Russian. You can order conveniently via the Internet, enter your telephone number, and you are called back for confirmation.

http://nn.delivery-club.ru/

SALT AND PEPPER

A very interesting idea hides behind this name. This is an offer for all who want to cook themselves, but do not feel like shopping. This website offers you the necessary ingredients and a recipe for a week.

www.solperets.ru

Night Life

You can find an overview of current events in Nizhny here:

http://kudago.com/nnv/

http://geometria.ru/nnov/announcements

You can buy tickets for events on the website *www.kassir.ru*. However, it is easier to get tickets at the respective pre-sale points (for example, in the shopping center "Etagé" or Bolshaya Pokrovskaya 18 - Б.Покровская, 18).

BU

The "Art-Café" is an alternative venue. Concerts are held at irregular intervals. You will find the announcements on the website.

Address: Zveszdinka Street 10/52 (ул. Звездинка 10/52)

http://bufet.su/

FABRIKA

As the name suggests, a rather rustic place. The restaurant at noon turns into a bar or disco with live music or DJs in the evening.

Opening hours: daily 11am-1am, Friday and Saturday till 6am
Address: Rozhdestvenskaya   Street   43   (ул. Рождественская, 43)

http://fabrikabar.ru/

FRANKY BAR

The stylishly furnished cocktail bar has an extensive selection of drinks.

Address: Zvezdinka Street 10 (ул. Звездинка, 10)

Opening hours: daily 12am-2am, Friday and Saturday till 6am

http://www.frankybar.ru/

LEX

The nightclub is open daily from 8pm to 5pm. Women usually have free admission. As in all Russian discos, there are go-go dancers.

http://www.lexxnn.ru/

MILO CLUB

The Milo Club is located on the sixth floor of the shopping center Etagé. Very futuristic decor and a nice view of the city. From 1pm to 11pm it is the White Café. In the evening, it turns into a discotheque.

Address: Belinskogo 63 (ул. Белинского 63, ТЦ "Этажи" 6 этаж)

http://milomilo.ru/

MILO CONCERT HALL

As the name suggests, this is a concert hall. But there are not only concerts. The venue is also used as a nightclub on the weekend. Usually only open on weekends.

Address: Rodionova Street 4 (ул. Родионова, 4)

http://miloconcerthall.ru/

MIXTURA

The bar has two floors. There is a small stage. Special events and live concerts take place on Fridays and Saturdays. Weekdays open from 7pm to 6am, on weekends from 8pm.

Address: Nizhnevolzhskaya Naberezhnaya 16 (Нижневолжская набережная, 16)

www.mixturabar.ru

NEGRONI BAR & ENOTECA

Italian kitchen. Opposite the comedy theater. Open daily from 12 noon. The bar is OK, but if you like wine, go to the small wine cellar – next to the entrance and down the stairs. However, it only opens at 7pm. A wide selection of wines. On Fridays wine tasting.

Address: Gruzinskaya Street 30 (Грузинская, 30)

PREMIO CENTER

Below the Kremlin wall on the Volga river there is the Premio complex consisting of the restaurant "Monet", a concert hall, and the discotheque "Indi-Club". The announcements for events can be found on the website.

Address: Nizhnevolzhskaya   Naberezhnaya   1B   (ул. Нижне-Волжская набережная, дом 1 «В»)

http://www.premiocentre.ru/

ROCKBAR

The name is a program. If you like rock music, this is the right place. Often live music on weekends.

Opening hours: Monday-Thursday 12am-2am

                 Friday 12am-5am

                 Saturday 1pm-5am

                 Sunday 1pm-2am

Address: Piskunova 11 (ул. Пискунова, 11)

http://rockbar.ru/

SKLAD

The Sklad club is part of the underground scene. It is located below the Kremlin in the halls of the former wine/vodka factory "Pochaina". The entrance is not easy to find. Everything is a little run down, but goes with the atmosphere. Open Friday and Saturday 10pm-9am.

Address: Pochainskaya Street17 (Почаинская, 17)

https://vk.com/skladclub

TEATRO

In the entertainment complex "Master Plaza" is the "Night Illusion Club T.E.A.T.R.O.". This is not only a discotheque, but is also used for concerts and other events, as it has a stage. The club is built like a theater.

Address: Maxim Gorky Street 141 (ул. Максима Горького, 141)

http://clubteatro.ru/

THE TOP CLUB

This beautiful villa from the 19th century is transformed on most Fridays and Saturdays from 11pm to a discotheque on two floors.

Address: Nizhnevolzhskaya Naberezhnaya 16 (Нижневолжская набережная, 16)

http://thetopclub.ru/

UNION JACK GRAND MUSIC PUB

In the style of a British pub with solid leather armchairs and a large bar spread over two floors. With live music at high volume, however, the pub turns more into a nightclub in the evening. Open daily from 12am to 2pm.

Address: Maxim Gorky Street 150 (ул. Максима Горького, 150)

http://unionjack.ru/grandmusicpub/

WATERDANCE FESTIVAL

Once a year, a techno festival takes place in the yacht club "Leto". Due to the location on the secluded Volga peninsula below the city, an undisturbed musical enjoyment is guaranteed over two days.

Address: Naberezhnaya Grebnogo Kanala 109 (Набережная Гребного канала, 109)

http://www.waterdance.ru/

Shopping

In the last 10 years the shopping centers in Nizhny have sprung up like mushrooms. Completely new and highly modern complexes have emerged. The shops are open every day and in general have very accommodating opening times. Some are even open around the clock. At every corner, there is also a "mom-and-pop grocery store" ("Produkty") or a small SPAR supermarket. The price level in Nizhny is comparable to an average European city. Often you ask yourself how the locals make it, considering that the average income is about 500€ monthly, and a pensioner receives about 10,000 rubles (about 150 €) a month. The exchange rate for the ruble has dramatically diminished in the last years compared to the Euro, which makes the prices from a European perspective somewhat cheaper.

BOOK STORE

DIRIZHABL

At the end of Bolshaya Pokrovskaya Street in the direction of Gorky Square there is a large bookstore (Дирижабль) over several floors.

http://www.dirigable-book.ru/

DOM KNIGI

Not far from the Trade Fair (Sovetskaya Street 14 - ул. Советская, 14) is the House of Books (Дом книги).

http://domkniginn.ru/

KNIZHNAYA GALEREYA

This bookshop specializes in foreign literature (German, English, Italian, French and Spanish). It is located in Volodarskogo Street 40 (ул. Володарского, 40 - Книжная Галерея).

http://books-gallery.ru/

LABIRINT

Labirint is exclusively an Internet business. The books will be delivered to your home within 5 days (minimum order 1600 rubles).

http://www.labirint.ru/

CHITAY GOROD

This chain has both a shop downtown as well as an Internet business. The entrance is somewhat hidden and from the outside it looks as if the shop was closed. (Piskunova 41 - ул. Пискунова, д.41).

http://www.chitai-gorod.ru/

UNIVERSITY BOOKSTORE

Both the Higher School of Economics (Bolshaya Pecherskaya 25/12 - ул. Большая Печерская, 25/12) and the Linguistic University (Minin Street 31a - ул. Минина, 31a), have bookshops offering foreign literature.

BUILDING SUPPLIES STORE

There is an Obi (http://www.obi.ru/decom/home.html) in the shopping center "Fantastika" as well as in the "Mega" with the usual assortment. In the shopping center "Sed'moe Nebo" there is also a Castorama (*http://www.castorama.ru/*).

CHRISTMAS TREE

New Year is celebrated in Russia like Christmas in Europe, with a Christmas tree and gifts. Due to that fact the Christmas tree sales in the city usually only open after Christmas. If you want to have a real Christmas tree in time you should order it on the Internet. This also has the advantage that it is delivered and, if desired, also put up. Christmas tree in Russian is called Yolka (ёлка). A Russian fir is comparatively cheap (from 1000 rubles). Unfortunately, it sheds many small needles. The popular Caucasian fir is much more expensive (from 5000 rubles – Пихта Нордмана).

http://elkalive.ru/

ETAGÉ

One of the first shopping centers in the city was "Etagé". It dates back to 2003. On the 6th floor is the Milo Club (see above "Night Life").

Address: Belinskogo Street 63 (ул. Белинского 63, ТЦ "Этажи")

http://www.etagi.ru/

FANTASTIKA

This shopping complex is one of the largest shopping centers in the city. In addition, there is an Obi, one of the largest cinemas in the city and a large fitness studio of the "Worldclass" chain.

Address: Rodionova Street 187 (ул. Родионова, 187)

http://fantastika-nn.ru/

FURNITURE STORE

The fastest way to furniture your home is, of course, with IKEA in the shopping center "Mega". If you have more time, you can order your furniture in an actual furniture store. A large selection is offered by "Otkryty Materik" (Larina 7, on the M7 towards the shopping center Mega – ул. Ларина, 7, "Открытый материк" http://materiknn.ru/) or "Mebelny Bazar" (Gordeevskaya 7a, not far from the railway station – ул. Гордеевская, 7a, "Мебельный базар"). With some persuasion, one can possibly get the items on display. There are no employees of the furniture store, but every furniture supplier is represented with his own sales representative, who operates a small exhibition space.

LOBACHEVSKY PLAZA

The luxury shopping center (Лобачевский Plaza) is located in the center of the city, not far from Bolshaya Pokrovskaya Street, with all high-priced brands and almost no customers. It has a car park in the middle of the city. Architecturally it is a modern building, so that it is worth a visit alone. It has an Apple Store, as well as a huge and high-priced children's store. And last but not the least, it has pizza in the Bocconchino (see above "Dining & Drinking").

Address: Alexeyevskaya Street 10/16 (ул. Алексеевская, 10/16)

MARKET

Especially in the summer, you get the freshest fruit in the market directly from Babushkas (grandmas). You should try to act as a local, since you will otherwise pay substantially more as a foreigner. A visit to a market is an experience at any time of the year. Bread, milk products, meat, fruit, vegetables, but also clothing are offered. However, the meat in most markets probably falls below European hygiene standards.

CENTRAL MARKET
The largest market of the city is located near the train station. (Chkalov Street 4 –улица Чкалова, 4).

KOMSOMOLKA
The largest covered market is just outside the other Oka shore. From the outside it looks more like a large modern supermarket. The interior is lined with small stands. It is open daily from 9am-9pm. (Komsomolskaya Square 6 – Комсомольская пл., 6 „КомсоМОЛка“).

http://komsomolka-nn.ru/

MYTNY DVOR
Directly at the beginning of Bolshaya Pokrovskaya Street (ул. Большая Покровская, 2 – Мытный двор) there is a small market, which has become even smaller in recent years. It is open daily from 7am to 7pm.

SREDNOY RYNOK

Not far from Lyadov Square there is a slightly larger market Srednoy on Kostina Street 13 (улица Костина, 13 - Средной). Here you can eat the best "Shaurma" (kebab) of the city (see above "Food & Drink").

MEGA

IKEA has made it to Nizhny. Around the stor a large shopping complex has emerged. It is about 20 km from the city center, however, and so you should plan about 45 minutes driving time without much traffic. The shopping center is open daily from 10am to 10pm. There is also the only Bosco shop in the city. **Bosco Sport** (https://boscosport.ru/) supplies athletes from the Olympics. The sportswear is expensive, but it is a nice souvenir.

www.megamall.ru

METRO

The "Metro" wholesale market is located in the suburbs on the other side of the Oka river behind the trade fair. Open every day from 7am to 11pm. There are some products here which would not be found in other supermarkets, but often only in large packaging.

Address: Meshersky Bulevard 3a (Мещерский бул., 3а)

https://nn.metro-cc.ru/

NEBO

This shopping center, opened in 2016, is the most recent in the city, right on Lyadov Square (Bolshaya Pokrovskaya 82 - Большая Покровская, 82). The first four hours parking in the underground parking are free of charge.

http://nebo-trk.com/

ONLINE SHOPPING

Online shopping is also very popular in Russia, but not always so simple and not so fast. Sometimes you pay for delivery to Nizhny and then again for the delivery to your home. There is a system called **Pickpoint**. The package is sent to a pick-up point, where you have to pay directly (http://pickpoint.ru/). The Russian version of Amazon is called **Ozon** (http://www.ozon.ru/). Looking for an Ebay-like site you should use "from hand to hand" ("**iz ruk v ruki**" http://irr.ru/). And the Russian variant of Google is **Yandex** (*https://www.yandex.ru/*).

RUSSIAN FASHION

RODINA

Rodina means homeland. This name is not chosen by chance. This business carries only Russian brands. Rodina also produces its own line of T-shirts and accessories. Open every day from 11am to 9pm. Address: Piskunova 9 (ул. Пискунова, 9).

http://rodinastore.ru/

ZARINA

Zarina is a women's fashion chain in the style of ZARA, spread throughout Russia. There are branches in the large shopping centers.

http://zarina.ru/

SOUVENIRS

The largest souvenir shop in the city is located on Bolshaya Pokrovskaya Street (Большая Покровская ул., 43) just before the end of the pedestrian zone in the direction of Gorky Square. Due to the striking red-yellow house front on the ground floor you cannot miss the building. Here you will find all the arts and crafts of the region. Even if you do not want to buy anything, it is well worth a visit.

Opening hours: daily 10am-8pm

An overview of all products can be found on the homepage: *http://russian-gift.com/*

SPORTING GOODS

REDFOX

To prepare for a trekking tour or other outdoor activities, this shop is just the thing. It is located on the first floor of the shopping center Novaya Era behind the train station in the direction of Moscow (Sormovskoye Avenue 20, Сормовское ш., 20, ТЦ Новая Эра, эт.

http://www.redfox.ru/

SNARYAZHENIE

This store also specializes in outdoor sports. Camping mats, tents, sleeping bags, and clothing from well-known suppliers. The small shop is located somewhat hidden next to the icerink "Dvorets Sporta" on Gagarina Avenue 29a (проспект Гагарина, 29А "Снаряжение"). They also rent **folding boats**.

http://www.equip.ru/

SPORTMASTER

This is the largest sporting activity store in the city. Here you will find everything from skiing to cycling, as well as clothing. A branch is located next to the shopping center "Etagé". The branch on Moskovskoye Avenue 105a (Московсковское ш., 105a) offers more choice.

http://www.sportmaster.ru/

TRIAL-SPORT

This store also has a wide selection. From the outside it appears somewhat unimpressive. Unfortunately no parking facilities (Sovetskaya Street 11 - ул. Советская, 11).

http://trial-sport.ru/

SUPERMARKET

You can buy food almost everywhere. The large supermarkets are of course not directly in the city center. The big chains are called Ashan, Billa, Karusel, Lenta, Metro, Okay, Perekrestok, Spar/Eurospar. They basically offer the same range of goods, with slight deviations. You get everything you need, though the selection of products is much narrower than in Europe. The Eurospar is very expensive, but it offers some products which are not available elsewhere.

TEA

Russia is known to be a tea drinking nation, but they favour mostly black or green tea. If you would like to have more choice, you should go to a tea shop, for example to the "teahouse" on Nesterova 3 (Чайный домик – ул. Нестерова, 3 – open daily from 9am to 9pm).

http://www.mendin.ru/

Hotels & Accommodation

As mentioned in other sections, living in Russia or vacationing there is not cheap. There are very nice apartments and hotels, but they have their price. If you want to rent an apartment, you should go over a broker. Most apartments are rented furnished. This is not to everyone's taste. Either the apartments are hypermodern, or alternatively come equipped with extremely heavy and dark furniture. The apartments in the upper price segment meet European standards. No one feels responsible for the entrance hall, for this reason it is in the best case untended. You should not be put off. If you do not want to live in a multi-family building in the city, you can possibly look for a house in a closed residential settlement outside the city. Remember, however, that there will be a lot of traffic on the roads to Nizhny in the morning and evening at the rush hour. As for hotels, most can be booked through booking.com. Another option is to rent a holiday home, with complete furnishings. This is especially convenient and recommended if you are traveling as a family with children.

ALEXANDROVSKY SAD

The hotel is located in the immediate vicinity of the park of the same name (see above "Parks and Lakes") and therefore not far from the Volga river. The modern complex with 50 rooms was built in 2004. A double room costs about 7000 rubles. The hotel has a bowling alley, sauna, pool and fitness room. The facilities can be used by non-hotel guests for a fee. For 1200-2300 rubles per hour you can also rent a separate sauna with pool to relax in complete privacy.

Address: Geogrievsky Syezd 3 (Георгиевский съезд,д.3)

http://www.achotel.ru/

DIPLOMAT HOTEL

A very decent and clean hotel with 33 rooms in a central location, within a 15-minute walk from the Kremlin. If you do not want to walk to the Kremlin, you can take a tram. There is a stop near the hotel. The hotel is mainly for business people, for this reason there are no big extras. The entrance is somewhat hidden. Walk past the restaurant Khurma (Хурма), and you will come across the entrance in the courtyard. Go to the 5th floor. A double room costs about 4000 rubles. The restaurant Khurma (Хурма) with the Azerbaijanian cuisine is recommended.

Address: Bolshaya Pecherskaya 26 (ул. Большая Печёрская, 26, эт. 5)

http://diplomat-hotel.ru/

FONDA

If you are looking for an extraordinary accommodation, this is the place to go. The small hotel with 6 rooms is a houseboat right on the Volga River. The hotel is part of a large sauna complex (see "Recreation and Sports" below). It is not possible to find a quieter place in the midst of a big city. The only downside: the hotel is not accessible by public transport. A double room costs 4000 rubles. For 15000 rubles you can rent a $120m^2$ apartment with a terrace, a fireplace, a billiard table and a private sauna. The rooms can also be rented by the hour if you want to relax after the sauna.

Address: Naberezhnaya Grebnogo Kanala 108 (Набережная Гребного канала, 108)

http://fonda52.ru/

GRAND HOTEL OKA

Located within about a15-minute drive from the city center, this large hotel complex has a bowling alley, fitness studio, large pool, sauna and wellness area. It is divided into two areas. The premium area is a modern 4-star hotel, and has 139 rooms. A single room is available from 5400 rubles. Large, but not quite cheap, suites can also be rented. The business area is much cheaper and corresponds to a 3-star hotel. In total, this side has 261 rooms. A double room starts at 1900 rubles. The complex is often used for large conferences. The complex also includes a jazz club "Jam Prestige" with a stage and live music (open from 5pm).

Address: Gagarina Avenue 27 (пр. Гагарина, д.27)

http://www.hoteloka.ru/

HOSTELS

FABRIKA

500 rubles in the 8-bed room; 1450 rubles per person in a double room. Common showers and toilets. Simple but clean. In many places the walls are unplastered. The red bricks give the hostel its flair. At the same time, the hostel serves as an art gallery. It is located in the lower part of the city center in a small side street of the pedestrian zone "Rozhdestvenskaya". At the corner there is a coffee shop of the chain "Coffee Cake".

Address: Rozhdestvenskaya   Street   24   (ул. Рождественская,24)

http://fabrika-hostel.ru/goroda/nizhnijnovgorod

SMILE HOSTEL

Bright, comfortable and furnished with attention to detail. Each room has the name of a large city and is individually designed. In the middle of the city at the beginning of Bolshaya Pokrovskaya Street. See for yourself through the visual 3D tour on the website. 390 rubles for a bed in the 8-bed room; 1490 rubles for a double room; Common showers and toilets.

Address: Bolshaya   Pokrovskaya   Street 4 (ул. Б. Покровская, 4)

http://smilehostel.net/en/

IBIS HOTEL

One of the largest hotels in the city center is the Ibis Hotel. This 3-star hotel has 220 rooms. The standard is the same as in Ibis hotels worldwide, and the rooms are neat and clean. You get a double room from about 3000 rubles.

Address: Maxim Gorky Street 115 (ул. Максима Горького, 115)

www.ibis.com

JOUK JACQUE

At the end of the pedestrian zone of Bolshaya Pokrovskaya there is a small hotel with 18 rooms. The cheapest double room costs 5200 rubles.

Address: Bolshaya Pokrovskaya Street 57 (ул. Б. Покровская, 57)

http://jak-hotel.com/

KULIBIN PARK HOTEL

Opened in 2015, this 4-star hotel is stylishly and modernly furnished in a brand new building right in the city center. A double room costs about 6000 rubles.

Address: Maxim Gorky Street 121 (ул. Максима Горького, 121)

http://kulibin-hotel.ru/

MARINS PARK HOTEL

This 450-room hotel, located near the center, is right next to the trade fair and the Oka River. It is on the opposite river side from the town center. Much of the hotel is newly renovated with modern rooms, but some rooms have not been updated. Make sure you have a renovated room with a view of the river. The hotel complex has two restaurants, a pub and a sauna. The standard double room costs 3300 rubles.

Address: Sovetskaya Street 12 (ул. Советская, д. 12)

http://www.hotel-central.ru/

MARRIOTT HOTEL

A very chic, new 4-star hotel with 143 rooms in the city center, opened in 2015. A 20-minute walk to the Kremlin. Prices are dependent on booking time and season – around 5000 rubles.

Address: Ilyinskaya Street 46 (ул. Ильинская, 46)

http://www.marriott.de/hotels/travel/gojcy-courtyard-nizhny-novgorod-city-center/

NIKOLA HOUSE

The hotel is located behind the drama theater, not far from Bolshaya Pokrovskaya Street and thus in the middle of the city and yet in a quiet location. The standard double room costs 6760 rubles. The hotel has a total of 31 rooms.

Address: Pozharsky Street 18 (ул. Пожарского, 18)

http://nikolahouse.com/

NINO HOTEL

A small, cheap, but clean hotel with a partial view of the Kremlin wall. The rooms do not all have private bathrooms. A double room with private bathroom costs 2490 rubles.

http://ninohotel.ru/

Address: Ilyinskaya Street 3 (ул. Ильинская, 3)

OKTYABRSKAYA HOTEL

If you want to enjoy an unobstructed view of the Volga from your room, you should book a room in this 3-star hotel directly on the traffic-free upper embankment. The hotel has 91 rooms. A standard double room costs 3700 rubles.

Address: Verkhnevolzhskaya Naberezhnaya 9a (Верхне-Волжская наб., 9a) *http://www.oktyabrskaya.ru/en/*

VOLNA

The best hotel close to the airport is the Hotel Volna. It is located about 9 km from the airport, close to the GAZ factory. A double room costs about 5100 rubles.

Address: Lenin Avenue 98 (пр. Ленина, 98)

www.volnahotel.ru

WHITE HOUSE

The hotel calls itself a "mini-hotel". The hotel is more of a hostel, but the rooms have their own bathroom. However, some rooms do not have a window. Single room from 1450 rubles. Extra charge for second person 100 rubles.

Address: Varvarskaya Street 27/8 (ул. Варварская, 27/8)

http://whhotel.ru/

Recreation and Sports

In this section you will learn about the many leisure and sports activities in Nizhny and surroundings.

BANYA

The Russian banya differs from the Finnish sauna. The air humidity is much higher, with higher temperatures at the same time. For this reason, some covering is usually worn to protect the hair. Water from a hot water tank is mixed with cold water in bowls and is used with a ladle for washing. In addition, it is customary to lightly beat the body with birch leaf bouquets to stimulate blood circulation. The banya is very popular and Russians who have "dachas" (summer houses) outside the city usually have a banya there as well. Try to get an invitation from your Russian friends. In the city center there are public banyas of varying quality. It is uncommon for women and men to go to the sauna together in public, at least not without bathing suits. There is a possibility to rent banyas by the hour. Though the larger hotels and fitness studios have Finnish and Turkish saunas.

BANYA NA NOVOY

A good and clean public sauna with small pool is located near Gorky Square on Novaya Street 13a. Three hours cost 470 rubles. Open daily (except Tuesdays) from 8am to 10pm. Wednesday, Friday, Sunday it is a men's sauna. Monday, Thursday, Saturday it is a women's sauna. If you do not want to use the public sauna, you can also rent a separate sauna room.

http://sauna-nn.ru/banya-na-novoy.html

USADBA VANNAYA

If you prefer luxury, but with the best location, you can rent a whole house, including a sauna, directly on the Volga River at Grebnoy Kanal Embankment 108/1 (наб. Гребного канала, 108/1). The complex is open around the clock and also has a small hotel. It is accessible however only by car. It is not cheap.

You need to reckon on about 7000 rubles for the two-hour minimum rental period.

http://bani52.ru/

BBQ

It is generally permitted to have a barbecue in parks. A beautiful opportunity in the city is the Shyolkovsky Hutor Park (see above "Parks and Lakes"). However, the fire risk is very high in the summer months, so the government often bans barbecues. Inquire beforehand to avoid a fine. If you want to be on the safe side, you can rent a nice barbecue place on a lake with facilities in Sormovsky Park. Environmental awareness is not yet very pronounced in Russia, so many people simply leave their garbage uncollected afterwards. Don't follow this example – show your love for the environment by disposing of your garbage.

BEACH VOLLEYBALL

Two beach volleyball courts are freely accessible on the city beach at Grebnoy Kanal. However, you must have your own net. In the summer, the pitches are always populated and you will find game partners without problems.

BOATING

Should you be in Nizhny in the summer, a boat trip on the Volga River is a must. There are different companies with different offers. You can tour the city from the water for 1-2 hours (about 350 rubles per person), or choose for example a day trip to Gorodets. There are also offers for several days of Volga boating. In addition, there is an option to rent a boat for private parties. Starting point is the Rechnoy Vokzal (see above "Sights – Rozhdestvenskaya Street). A good company is Vodokhod (ВодоходЪ), which has an office in the Rechnoy Vokzal.

http://volga-vodohod.ru/river-walks/

CABLE CAR

The ride with the cable car over the Volga River takes about 20 minutes. You can enjoy a nice view. A trip is therefore recommended both in the summer and in the winter. However, there is not much to see on the other side.

CAMPING

In Russia there are very few official camping sites. It is, however, allowed to camp in the forest. However, be aware of possible restrictions on open fires as the risk of fire is high in summer.

DANCING

Nizhny has dance clubs for standard and Latin American dances, and recently many different dance schools have been established. Here are just a few examples:

Salsa School „Milange"

Address: Zvezdinka 24 (Звездинка, 24)

http://salsann.ru/

Standard and Latin American Dances

Dance school by Anton Efremov, who is himself an active dancer

Address: Alexeyevskaya Street 8/1 – 5th floor (Алексеевская, 8/1, 5 этаж)

https://vk.com/must_dance

Te Amo – Dance School

Right in the pedestrian zone there is a dance school for salsa and other dances.

Address: Bolshaya Pokrovskaya Street 22 (ул. Большая Покровская, д. 22)

http://www.teamodance.ru/

FITNESS STUDIO

Russia has also embraced the fitness trend. There are new fitness studios everywhere. The newest club with a large pool and spa area is located in the shopping center Nebo (see above "shopping"). The largest chains are Worldclass and Fizkult with several clubs throughout the city – mostly in the large shopping centers. With an annual membership, there is the option to use different studios of the same chain. It is a bit cheaper to limit the membership to one studio. The larger studios have a large swimming pool and a Finnish and a Turkish sauna. The fitness equipment is modern. The selection of courses is usually great. For children from three years of age, there is usually child care. There are also courses specially for parents with children.

http://fizkult-nn.ru/

http://www.worldclass-nn.ru/

ICE SKATING

Ice skating and ice hockey are incredibly popular sports in Russia. Even the smallest children are on skates. It is therefore not surprising that there is even an ice rink in the shopping center Mega (see above "shopping") (1,5h cost 100 rubles).

DYNAMO STADIUM

In the winter, you can go ice-skating in the center of the city, in the "Dynamo" stadium.

Open daily from 4pm-9:30pm. Monday closed.

Entrance costs 50 rubles. Renting skating shoes costs 100 rubles per hour.

SORMOVSKY PARK

The indoor ice rink in Sormovsky Park can be used all year round. Ice skates can be rented on site (size 27-47, 150 rubles). You cannot pay cash, and have to use the machine for tickets. For this you need a plastic card for the park, which you buy at the machine and which must be charged with money. But beware, the machine does not provide change. If you do not have change, you can also pay at the cash desk diagonally opposite the entrance. A ticket costs 200 rubles without any time limit.

Opening hours: Monday 10am-7:30pm; Tuesday 10am-4pm +
6pm-10pm; Wednesday 10am-6pm; Thursday
10am-10pm; Friday 10am-5:30pm + 6:30pm-
10pm; weekend 12am-10pm

http://sormovopark.ru/rink

PADDLING

In the sport shop Snaryazhenie (see above "Shopping – sporting goods"), folding boats can be rented. If you have an option to transport a plastic boat, this is of course the easiest for a day trip. For day trips we recommend a trip to the river Linda, about an hour from Nizhny. Drive over the first Volga bridge to Rekshino (Рекшино). This is a good place to start. Remember that you need a car at the beginning and at the end of the route, or someone to pick you up again.

SEGWAY

If you do not want to walk, you can try a Segway. A ride on a Segway will cost 150 rubles for 5 minutes.

http://prokatsegway.ru/rent

SWIMMING POOLS

Public swimming pools can only be used with a medical certificate (Spravka). Inquire at the swimming pool you prefer. A very good public swimming pool is located in the large sport complex Meshera (Karl Marx street 17a / ул. Карла Маркса 17a "Мещера"). If you want to go swimming without a doctor's certificate, you can either go to Grandhotel Oka (see above "Hotels & Accommodation") or use a membership in one of the large fitness studios (see above).

SWIMMING LAKES

In the park Shyolkovsky Hutor (see above "Parks and Lakes") there is a small sandy beach and partly a lawn for sunbathing at both lakes. The water quality unfortunately, is questionable. The locals swim there, but they also swim in the Volga at the city beach (Grebnoy Kanal) and this certainly is not recommended. This is also true for the lakes in Sormovsky Park and for the Mesherskoye Ozero near the shopping center "Sedmoye Nebo".

North on the M7 (direction Moscow) there are several swimming lakes. Consult a map. They are usually clean and you can camp nearby. However, you have to bring everything you need, as there are no shopping facilities nearby. Be careful where you park, since the soil is very sandy and you can easily get stuck. Suggestions: Svetlye Ozera (Светлые озера) or Ozero Pyrskoye (озеро Пырское).

SKIING

The winter is long, cold and snowy. Unfortunately, Nizhny lacks mountains, so that only cross-country skiing is recommended. If you have your own skis, you can ski almost in any park in Nizhny. If you are looking for groomed tracks, then you will find them in Shyolkovsky Hutor Park . There are also several ski rental shops. On weekends, however, the crowds in the park are big.

Ski rental: Koreyskaya Street 22 (Корейская улица, 22); Daily from 9am to 6pm; 200 rubles. You must deposit your passport as security.

If however, you prefer downhill, there are a few small hills and a little further away from Nizhny, some small ski resorts.

HABARSKOYE

About 40km away from Nizhny towards Bogorodsk is the ski complex "Habarskoye" (Хабарское) on the Oka. Ski rental, three lifts and hotel on site.

http://www.habarskoe.ru/

NOVINKI

About 7km away from Nizhny in the direction of Bogorodsk, on the Oka River, there is the nearest ski lift in Novinki. Everything is new and modern with a lift and two slopes. There is also a practice slope and a ski rental.

http://www.novinki-nn.ru/

SWITZERLAND PARK

The closest opportunity for downhill skiing with a small lift is the skiing center "Na Sludye" (На Слуде) below the Switzerland Park. It is not so easy to find. Before the park starts, turn right in front of the petrol station and follow the road to the Oka. Turn left and you will come across the ski slope. Open on weekends 10am-4pm; Tuesday and Thursday from 2pm to 4pm. Use of the cableway 200-400 rubles.

PUZHALOVA

About 80km on the M7 towards Moscow there is this ski resort with 6 runs.

http://www.puzhalova.ru/

TERRA SKI PARK

About 40km on the M7 (direction Kazan) is this ski resort which opened in 2016. Two lifts, 5 slopes and a practice slope.

http://www.terraskipark.ru/

TENNIS

In the center of the city, not far from the Kremlin, there is a tennis club with several outdoor courts. It is located behind the restaurant "Sportsbar" (Piskunova 40e – ул. Пискунова, 40e)

http://unionsport-nn.ru/

If you want to play tennis all year round, you can do so in the large, brand new and covered tennis park (Gagarina Avenue 33 – просп. Гагарина, 33).

http://tennispark-nn.ru/

YACHT CLUB

If you have your own boat or rent a boat to go on the Volga, you can choose one of the various yacht clubs:

http://yachtclub-nn.ru/

http://www.katernn.ru/yacht-club.html

http://www.fps-nn.ru/

http://www.katernn.ru/

http://jordan.com.ru/

YOGA

Yoga is also popular in Russia. A large yoga center is the eco-center "Miraya" (Alexeyevskaya Street 41g – Ул. Алексеевская, д.41 г). They also offer a group for parents with babies and yoga especially for pregnant women, children and a rehabilitation course.

http://miraya.ru/

Travelling with children

Russia is extremely child-friendly. In almost every restaurant there are play corners and some even have child care.

BABY CONCERT NN

An extraordinary concept, especially for children up to 5 years. Classical music for the little ones to touch. A small ensemble plays well-known classical music. There is child care available. The dates can be found on the website. 800 rubles for one parent plus child. Address: Beketova Street 13K (ул. Бекетова, 13К, 5 этаж (МЦ "БУМ").

http://babyconcertnn.ru/

BABY SWIMMING

Baby swimming is very popular in Russia. A nice pool available for children from 2 months to 7 years can be found in the children's clinic Zdorovyonok (Детская клиника Здоровёнок)

Address: Vorovskogo Street 22 / ул. Воровского, 22).

You need a bathing permit (Spravka) for yourself and your child, which should be issued by a doctor.

http://zdorovenok.sadkomed.ru/bassein

CIRCUS

A great new building on the Oka bank near the train station. There are no permanent ensembles, but guest performances by foreign circus groups. The only difference is that the circus tent is a solid building.

Address: Kommunisticheskaya Street 38 (ул. Коммунистическая, 38)

http://www.circus-nnovgorod.ru/

CRAFT SHOP

The large shop "Leonardo" is located in the shopping center Fantastika, and also the shopping center Nebo.

http://leonardohobby.ru/ishop/

FAMILY CENTER „GREENLANDIA"

The center has offerings for the whole family. There are courses for parents, a half-day nursery and a salt cave.

Address: Volodarskogo Street 38a – улица Володарского, 38А

http://www.greenlandia-nn.ru/

FUN FAIR

Both Sormovsky Park and Switzerland Park (see above "Parks and Lakes") have a fun fair all summer with various rides. There is a big ferris wheel (entrance from Meditsinskaya Street), a chairoplane, a go-cart track (entrance from Surikov Street) and much more.

GO-KART TRACK

In the Sormovsky Park (see above "Parks and Lakes") there is a small go-kart track with four cars for adults and two for children. Open from 10am to 10pm. On weekends, children ride for 250 rubles (5 minutes).

INDOOR PLAYGROUNDS

In many shopping centers, there are children's playgrounds not only at IKEA's. Since the winter is quite long, this is a good alternative for cold weather days.

IZUMRUDNY GOROD

The "Emerald City" has two locations in Nizhny – one in the shopping center Gansa, and another in the shopping center Burnakovsky.

Opening hours: daily 10am-9pm

Price:	30 minutes 200 Rubel; children under 3 years must be accompanied by an adult (30 min. 50 rubles)
Address:	Shopping center Gansa, Rodionova Street 165/13 (ТЦ Ганза, Родионова ул., 165 к.13) Shopping center Burnakovsky, Burnakovskaya Street 55 (ТЦ Бурнаковский, Бурнаковская ул., 55)

http://www.iz-gorod.com/

MURAVEYNIK

Children over the age of one can have a good romp in the "Anthill" in the "Nebo" shopping center and in the shopping center "Mega" (see above "shopping"). You can also leave the children there to go shopping yourself in peace.

Opening hours: daily 10am-10pm

Price: 250 rubles weekdays; 350 rubles on weekends per hour; accompanying person is free of charge

http://muravejnik.com/

OSTROV SOKROVISH′

The "Treasure Island" (Остров сокровищ) is located in the shopping center Gagarinsky (ТЦ Гагаринский). 300 rubles during the week; 350 rubles on weekends.

Address: Gagarin Avenue 105a (просп. Гагарина, 105a).

MUSEUM OF SCIENCE – KVARKI

A well-made museum – sciences to touch. Many experiments to try out for yourself. The entrance to the museum is at the back of the trade fair building. Open every day from 10am to 7pm. Entrance at the weekend 350 rubles.

Address: Sovnarkomovskaya Street 13 (ул. Совнаркомовская, 13)

OPERA AND BALLET THEATER

The Opera House offers a special children's program. About one event per month. Recommended for children from 3 years and up.

Address: Belinskogo Street 59/2 (улица Белинского, 59/2)

http://operann.ru/

PLAYGROUNDS

In almost every park in the city center there is a playground, usually new and well maintained. Also on Bolshaya Pokrovskaya there is a nice playground. However, there is always a great crowd.

PONY RIDING

On nice days, children can ride small ponies (guided by hand) on Bolshaya Pokrovskaya (about 200 rubles).

PUPPET THEATER

The building is fabulously designed, with four small pointed roofs including weather flags. Various programs for different ages.

Address: Bolshaya Pokrovskaya 39b (Большая Покровская улица, 39б)

http://www.ngatk.ru/

STADIUM VODNIK

The stadium (Водник) is somewhat hidden in a residential area in the center, between Osharskaya and Alexeyevskaya streets. In the summer, the locals spend their time cycling, jogging, inline skating or playing football.

TOY MUSEUM

It looks more like a flea market than a museum. A visual tour is available on the website.

Address: Bolshaya Pokrovskaya Street 8 (ул. Б. Покровская, 8)

http://www.ngiamz.ru/filialy/vystavochnyj-zal-pokrovka-8.html

WATERPARK „CARIBBEAN"

In the Sormovsky Park (see above "Parks and Lakes") there is a small leisure and fun pool. Heated pool (at 28 degrees), water depth 1.40m, five water slides (2 for adults, 3 for children).

Opening hours: in summer 10am-10pm

Price: 300 rubles during the week; 350 rubles on weekends

http://sormovopark.ru/aquapark

YOUTH THEATER

The program here is specially designed for children and teenagers. The current program can be viewed on the Internet.

Address: Maxim Gorky Street 145 (Театр юного зрителя – улица Максима Горького, 145)

http://www.tyuz.ru/

ZOO LIMPOPO

A completely restored zoo on the edge of Sormovsky Park. There is a pay parking at the entrance. Since 2015 there is even a giraffe. Includes a beautiful petting zoo.

Entrance fee: 400 rubles

Address: Yaroshenko Street 7b (ул. Ярошенко, 7б)

http://www.nnzoo.ru/

Church Services

BAPTIST

Service: Sundays 10am and 5pm

Address: Poltavsky Pereulok 10 (Полтавский переулок, 10)

CATHOLIC CHURCH

The three nuns of the church also run the Caritas, which every weekday at noon provides lunch to the needy. Helping hands are always sought. Occasionally, a Taizé prayer takes place on a Friday evening.

Service: Sundays 12 noon, Saturdays 6pm pre-evening mass

Address: Studyonaya Street 10b (Студёная улица, 10Б)

http://cathon.org/index_eng.htm

EVANGELICAL CONGREGATIONS

JESUS EMBASSY CHURCH

The largest evangelical congregation in Nizhny is the Jesus Embassy Church. The pastor of the church is Pavel Ryndich. There is a separate service in English, which is mainly attended by foreign students. Modern worship music with a band. Many young people attend. Donations can also be made by debit card. The Sunday service is broadcast live on the church's website.

Service: Sundays 11am and 1pm

Address: 50-let Pobedy Street 18 (улица 50-летия Победы, 18)

http://en.jesusembassy.org/

VINEYARD CHURCH

The congregation was founded by missionaries from America and has been headed by them until 2017. For this reason, worship is usually available in both English and Russian. Modern worship singing at the beginning of the service. Small community with about 60 members, some of them from abroad. The service is in the middle of the city on the first floor of the Sverdlov Cultural Center in the pedestrian zone.

Service: Sundays 11:30am; in English and Russian

Address: Bolshaya Pokrovskaya 18 (Большая Покровская улица, 18).

http://vcfnn.org/

LUTHERAN CHURCH

The church has a small organ, so that occasional concerts are held. See the vKontakte page for more information.

Service: Sundays 12 noon

Address: Slavyanskaya Street 39 (Славянская улица, 39)

http://elc-nn.jimdo.com/

https://vk.com/ingriann

MOSQUE

Address: Kasanskaya Naberezhnaya 6 (Казанская набережная, 6)

http://www.islamnn.ru/

SYNAGOGUE

The synagogue can be visited Monday to Friday from 9am to 6pm and Sunday from 10am to 3pm.

Address: Gruzinskaya Street 5a (ул. Грузинская, 5а)

http://www.evreinn.ru/

Kindergarten, Schools and Universities

HIGHER SCHOOL OF ECONOMICS

This university has a small "Austrian" library. There are Russian language courses, various summer schools and an international master program.

Address: Bolshaya Pecherskaya 27 (Большая Печёрская улица, 27)

https://nnov.hse.ru/en/

KINDERGARTEN

For a place in the Russian nursery, you probably have to register your child at birth. However, there are some very good private nurseries.

CREF

For children aged 2-7 years. Trilingual (Russian, English, French). Foreign languages are taught by native speakers.

Address: Dalnaya Street 11 (ул. Дальняя 11)

http://nnovgorod.ptitcref.com/en/

KROKHA

There is a variety of private, Russian kindergartens. The education of children is very important. The quality of child care and the programs is very good. The nursery "Krokha" is just one example.

Address: Gruzinskaya Street 37a (ул. Грузинская, 37a)

http://kroha52.ru/

DOBROLYUBOV STATE LINGUISTICS UNIVERSITY

Russian classes are available here for foreigners. In addition, there is a test center for the Russian language test, which has been obligatory since 2015 for some long-term visas.

Address: Minin Street 31a (ул. Минина, 31a)

http://www.lunn.ru/

http://www.lunn.ru/page/centr-testirovaniya

LOBACHEVSKY STATE UNIVERSITY

The Lobachevsky University is the largest university in the city. There are also special programs for foreigners.

http://www.unn.ru/

LOMONOSOV INTERNATIONAL PRIVATE SCHOOL

This private school claims to be "international". However, there are few expats with children in Nizhny, so there are few foreign children at school. But the school certainly has many programs, all at a high level, with a price to match. Be aware, however, that only the children of the rich locals go here.

Address: Gogol Street 62 (ул. Гоголя, 62)

http://www.ils.education/index.php?menu=about&lang=ru&lang=en

STATE MEDICAL ACADEMY

Anyone who wants to study medicine in Russia can even do this partially in English at the Medical University.

http://www.nizhgma.ru/eng/

Medical Services

It is certainly better not to get sick at all. Some of the expats living here also categorically say that you must go to Moscow for any serious medical treatment. However, this is not always necessary. The doctors are well educated in Russia, and there are private clinics. Especially in the field of dental medicine, the costs are much lower compared to Europe, and with the same quality.

BIRTHING CLINIC

The birthing clinics in Russia are separate from the hospital. In Russia, it is not common for men to participate in the birth. Rather, women are handed over at the door and picked up a few days later with a child. Visitors not allowed during the stay. One of the better clinics is Birth Clinic No. 1 (Vavarskaya Street 42 – Родильный дом № 1 – ул. Варварская, 42), in the center. However, the standards are probably not what you are used to. There are few private rooms, but whether they are available, of course, cannot be guaranteed. For giving birth it´s recommended to go to Moscow. As a private patient, you are in good hands in a state's birth clinic.

http://www.ncagip.ru/ (ФГБУ Научный центр акушерства, гинекологии и перинатологии имени академика В.И. Кулакова – г. Москва, ул. Академика Опарина, дом 4)

http://rod-dom1.ru/

PEDIATRICIAN

A very good children's clinic is the clinic "Zdorovyonok". Everything is up-to-date. However, there is a specialist for everything and blood tests must be taken for each vaccination. The service is impeccable. No waiting time and a small playground is included. Open every day from 9am to 6pm. The clinic also offers a translator who speaks English.

Address: Vorovskogo Street 22 (ул. Воровского, 22)

http://zdorovenok.sadkomed.ru/

For serious emergencies, it is recommended to go to the children's hospital of the region (ГБУЗ НО Нижегородская областная детская клиническая больница). However, this is not nearly at the standard you might be used to. It begins with the challenge of finding the entrance. You should call the emergency to request an ambulance.

Address: Vaneeva Street 211 (ул. Ванеева, 211)

PRIVATE CLINIC

One of the largest private clinics is the "Sadko" clinic. This is not a hospital, but a medical center with all the specialties, including dentists. There are translators for English and French. The various clinics are spread all over the city.

http://eng.sadkomed.ru/

Excursions

If you have a longer stay in Nizhny, it is worth also exploring the surroundings, both in the Oblast (region) and beyond. Here are a few recommendations. In the following link there are other excursion destinations with detailed descriptions – but everything only in Russian (http://klubok-ok.ru/Nizheg.obl/Nizh_obl.html). For the more remote excursions, there is little information on site, and you will be lucky to find what you are looking for.

ARSAMAS

Arsamas is a small town 100km south of Nizhny. It takes about 2 hours by car. There are some beautiful churches to visit. The most beautiful and extraordinary church is in the center. With the columns and domes it could just as well be in Rome. Certainly worth a trip.

GORKOVSKOYE MORE

About 70km north west of Nizhny is a large reservoir on the Volga River. It is surrounded by countless holiday parks with hotels, full board, private beach and leisure programs (база отдыха). A high-quality facility is Izumrudnoye (http://izumrudnoe.ru/), which is located about two hours by car from Nizhny on the eastern side of the reservoir. Recommended both in summer and winter.

GORODETS

This small town is just outside the reservoir. A day trip by boat is recommended. There is a small samovar museum. Gorodets is also known for its gingerbread. Directly on the shore is a large wooden building, where the craftsmanship of the region is shown and souvenirs are sold.

ICHALKOVSKIE CAVES

Not easy to find, but in any case worth a visit. The caves are situated in a forest about 2 hours south of Nizhny (Ичалковские пещеры). Do not forget your flashlight.

KASAN

Kazan is located 400km east of Nizhny, also on the Volga river and is the capital of the autonomous Republic of Tatarstan. A beautiful city that is very Muslim, with a large mosque in the center of the Kremlin. Tatarstan is very rich because of its petroleum. This is evident in the city center and buildings. The Ministry of the Environment is particularly impressive, with a large artificial tree in its entrance, illuminated beautifully at night.

MAKARYEV MONASTERY

The Makaryev Monastery (Макарьевский монастырь) is located about 100 km from Nizhny, directly on the Volga. You should cross the Volga to get to it. The only available bridge is the bridge in Nizhny in the direction of Bor, but you can take a ferry in both Nizhny and Lyskovo (Лысково). The ferry lands directly in front of the monastery. From the water, you have a beautiful view of the monastery.

Ferry times:

From Lyskovo to Makaryevo: 06:15am, 08:15am, 12:15am, 3:15pm, 6:15pm.

From Makaryevo to Lyskovo: 7am, 9am, 1pm, 4pm, 7pm.

However, you should check the ferry times by telephone before the trip (8-930-802-99-59).

RUKAVISHNIKOVS' SUMMER RESIDENCE

South of the Oka River, about 100km from Nizhny, near Bogorodsk, is the ruin of the Rukavishnikov summer residence (Усадьба Приклонских-Рукавишниковых). The Rukavishnikov Villa in the center of the city is one of the most beautiful houses and is located on the Verkhnevolzhskaya Naberezhnaya (see above "Sights"). In the summer it is not easy to find. You need an off-road car, since the last part is only a dirt road. Do not drive after it rains, since there is a risk of getting stuck. On arrival, you will be rewarded with a great view of the Oka. The building itself is rather rundown, and a visit is only possible around the exterior, but one can picture the property as it once was. Entrance costs 200 rubles. You must ring at the gate. One family has devoted themself to preserving and rebuilding the estate. A guided tour is interesting, but it is only available in Russian.

http://usadbann.ru/

SEMYONOV

A must in Russia is the visit to the Matryoschka factory. It is located about 80km north of Nizhny. Semyonov has been the center of the famous Khokhloma wood art since the 17th century. Since 1930, the famous Matryoshkas have been produced here. Occupational safety is not a matter of top priority in the factory, and it is frightening under what conditions work is done. The machines are very old and one can hardly believe that such beautiful works of hand-painted art can come from this shabby factory. In any case, everything is handmade. If you plan to visit the factory, you must make an appointment beforehand (831-62) 2-22-72. Otherwise you will only have the museum and the souvenir shop to visit.

SUZDAL

Suzdal belongs to the so-called Golden Ring around Moscow and is one of the most important tourist destinations in Russia. The city is very touristy, but the many churches are beautifully restored and an excursion worthwhile in any case. By car you need at least 3.5 hours. Therefore, you should plan an overnight stay while visiting Vladimir, too.

SVETLOYAR

If you continue to Semyonov for another 40km, you will arrive at Svetloyar Lake. The lake is in the middle of a nature reserve and is very clean, so you can also swim there. It is one of the largest and deepest lakes in the region. There is a camp ground nearby. Campfire and tents directly at the lake side are forbidden. Every year, on 6th of July, there is a folk festival. Candles are lit at night. It is said that if one runs around the lake three times with a candle, a wish comes true.

About the Author

I came to Russia for the first time in 2005, to do a one-month internship at the Linguistic University in Nizhny Novgorod. At that time, I had no idea that seven years later I would be back, to work and to spend four and a half years there with my family. My knowledge of Russian was rudimentary, which did not make life easy at first because there is only a  small international community in Nizhny compared to centers such as Moscow and St. Petersburg. I dedicated myself to learning Russian, and to exploring the city. The idea for this travel guide came about when my Russian friends thought I was getting to know Nizhny better than they did! This guide does not claim to be complete, but reflects my experiences in both Nizhny and its surroundings. I had a wonderful time in Russia, and I owe this above all to the Russian warmth and hospitality. Embrace the people and the culture, and Nizhny will receive you with open arms.

The book was originally written in German. My friend **Leslie A. Pal** was so kind to translate the guide book into English. He is a professor at Carlton University, Ottawa, Canada. In 2012 we attended a summer school in Russian language studies together in Nizhny and he enjoyed being guided through the city by me.